MURDERS OF LONDON

D0543483

30 28 80060 690 0

Published by Random House Books 2012

2 4 6 8 10 9 7 5 3 1

Copyright © David Long 2012

David Long has asserted his right under the Copyright, Designs
and Patents Act, 1988, to be identified as the author of this work

All location photographs are courtesy of the author. We also gratefully
acknowledge DB-Photography, Justin Goring and Aleister Kelman for allowing
the use of their images under Creative Commons Attribution 2.0 licensing.

First published in Great Britain in 2012 by
Random House Books
Random House, 20 Vauxhall Bridge Road,
London SW1V 2SA

www.randomhouse.co.uk

Addresses for companies within The Random House Group Limited
can be found at: www.randomhouse.co.uk/offices.htm

The Random House Group Limited Reg. No. 954009

A CIP catalogue record for this book
is available from the British Library

ISBN 9781847946720

The Random House Group Limited supports The Forest Stewardship
Council® (FSC®), the leading international forest certification organisation.
Our books carrying the FSC label are printed on FSC® certified paper.
FSC is the only forest certification scheme endorsed by the leading
environmental organisations, including Greenpeace. Our paper procurement
policy can be found at www.randomhouse.co.uk/environment

Designed and produced by
The Curved House/Jim Smith

Printed and bound in China by C&C Offset Printing Co Ltd

DAVID LONG

MURDERS OF LONDON

IN THE STEPS OF THE CAPITAL'S KILLERS

CONTENTS

INTRODUCTION

EVERYONE LOVES A GOOD MURDER.

Just as in the past the public used to crowd around the gallows, sinking pints of ale and watching gruesome executions, people today will pay good money to sit in a darkened room with a bucket of popcorn while enjoying the latest graphically violent thriller. It is true that traditional, old-fashioned sleuthing and inspired guesswork have been usurped by the increasingly sophisticated science of forensics, but there is nothing new about our fascination with murderers – in the past racehorses, greyhounds and even a ship have been named after the most notorious – nor any sign that this is diminishing.

Of course murders happen all the time, and only a minority of them have that special attribute needed to command our attention. When that happens the media is skilled at playing its part in whipping up public interest, and crime reporters have a long history of rearranging the facts in order to construct a more compelling narrative. As long ago as 1847, for example, several newspapers famously ran breathless accounts of the dignified courtroom composure of murderess Mary Ann Milner – despite her having been found hanging in her cell the previous day.

Even without this kind of encouragement, however, the urge to glimpse a killer in the flesh and see justice done has always been strong. Around the same time as Milner's trial, a German visitor to London was told by a woman he met during his stay, 'You wish to know where the people's merry-makings are held? Go to Newgate on a hanging day – There you will find shouting, and joking, and junketting, from early dawn until the hangman has made his appearance and performed his office.'

On such occasions great stands would be erected for spectators, and landlords of taverns fortunate enough to occupy sites overlooking the scaffold would charge a premium for their beer and brandy, well in excess of what Londoners would have stood for on an ordinary weekday. Spectators of both sexes, every age and all classes thronged the streets in the hope of witnessing an actual execution.

Today we like to think we are more civilised than this, yet the attraction – 'enjoyment' really might not be too strong a word for it – has never really gone away. The decision to abandon public hangings was deeply unpopular; so too was the abolition of capital punishment in 1965; and lifelike waxworks of serial killers and other murderers have always numbered among Madame Tussaud's most popular attractions.

Indeed, even now, many decades after their conviction and imprisonment or execution, London's worst murderers find themselves as celebrated as any of the city's more talented or public-spirited inhabitants. Names such as Crippen, Christie and Ellis – and of course Jack the Ripper – are woven into the fabric of London's cultural history, alongside those of Whittington, Dickens and Wren. While most visitors to the capital still seek out the likes of St Paul's, the Tower and the Bank of England, many others will pore over books and maps looking to pinpoint such infamous addresses as 10 Rillington Place, 39 Hilldrop Crescent or Whitechapel's notorious Blind Beggar pub.

This book is for them, the ones who want to see for themselves a darker side of this great city, and to explore some of the more macabre episodes in its long and blood-soaked history.

DAVID LONG, 2012

WWW.DAVIDLONG.INFO

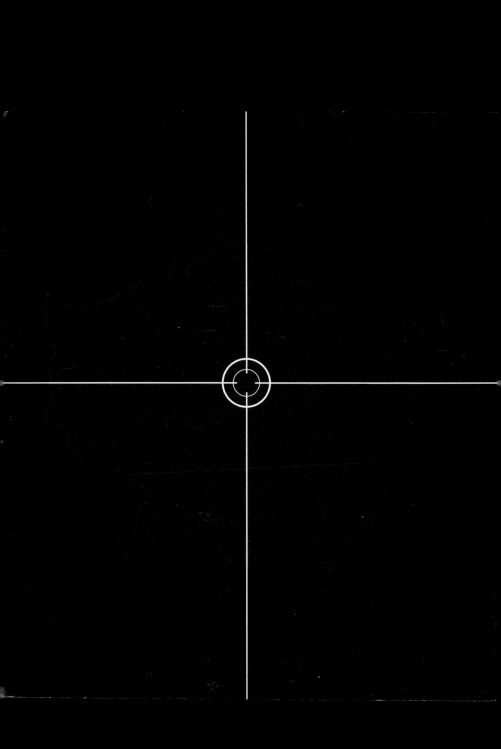

EAST OF THE CITY 1

MURDERS OF LONDON

JOHN WILLIAMS
AND THE RATCLIFFE HIGHWAY MURDERS (1811)

- **29 THE HIGHWAY, E1**
- **CANNON STREET ROAD/CABLE STREET CROSSROADS, E1**
- **CINNAMON STREET, E1**

UNTIL THE ABOLITION OF EXECUTION in Britain, it was standard practice for convicted murderers to be buried without ceremony beneath the prisons at which they died. Between 1902, when Pentonville took over from Newgate as London's very own death row, and the last execution in Britain in 1964, an estimated 119 bodies – including those of Dr Crippen (p.136) and John Christie (p.240) – were interred beneath the prison's gardens.

Occasionally, however, certain convicts were singled out for special treatment, but very rarely with the gruesome glee that seems to have attended the occasion in 1811 when the remains of John Williams were consigned to an especially bleak spot in East London.

Williams was widely believed to be the perpetrator of a series of bloody killings that came to be called the Ratcliffe Highway Murders. The first was committed at what is now 29 The Highway: the original building is long gone, although a wealth of old warehouses and wharf buildings still give some indication of how this dockside area might have looked in the early nineteenth century.

29 THE HIGHWAY

CINNAMON STREET

CANNON STREET ROAD /
CABLE STREET CROSSROADS

In 1811 no.29 was a hosiery business whose owner, 24-year-old Timothy Marr, lived on the premises with his wife and child. On the evening of 7 December he asked the servant girl, Margaret, to go out for some oysters; on her return she found the family and one of the shop's apprentices dead. All had had their throats cut and their heads staved in using a bloody ship's hammer or maul, which was recovered at the scene.

To avoid panic in the tight knot of surrounding streets, the authorities quickly rustled up the offer of a £500 reward for the murderer's capture, this at a time when the governor of the Bank of England received just £400 per year. It was generous, but to no avail, and exactly two weeks later at the King's Arms tavern in what is now Glamis Road, the landlord, John Williamson, was similarly done to death together with his wife, Elizabeth, and Bridget Harrington, who helped behind the bar. On this occasion there was a witness, a lodger who managed to escape from a back bedroom by climbing down a sheet he had knotted to the window.

With the public clamouring for some firm action, the authorities soon announced a number of arrests, sufficient in number that one of them – of a seaman called John Williams, apprehended on 21 December in Cinnamon Street – aroused no particular interest. He had been seen drinking in the King's Arms and after being interviewed by Shadwell magistrates was remanded in custody at Coldbath Fields Prison in Clerkenwell. (The site is now occupied by the giant Mount Pleasant Sorting Office.)

The evidence against Williams was extremely slim and 200 years later his guilt is by no means certain. He was found with a knife and was a fairly disreputable character but neither of these would have marked him out from many of the residents of this part of London at the time. He was also nothing like the description of the large man seen fleeing the scene by the Williamsons' lodger, being altogether rather less substantial.

The authorities were nevertheless content that they had caught their man, and were thus shocked to find Williams hanging in his cell on 27 December, the date on which he had been due to undergo further questioning. Suicide was at this time an illegal act, and by taking matters into his own hands Williams had also denied the courts and the public the opportunity to see justice being done.

ALL HAD HAD THEIR THROATS CUT AND THEIR HEADS STAVED IN USING A BLOODY SHIP'S HAMMER OR MAUL

In the absence of a usefully cathartic trial it was decided to parade Williams's corpse through Wapping and Shadwell, in part to reassure the local population that it had no more to fear but also in some way to avenge the dead. A procession duly set off on New Year's Eve, pausing for a few minutes at each crime scene and gradually attracting a crowd of more than 10,000 who wished to enjoy the gruesome spectacle.

It had also been decided to give Williams a traditional suicide's burial; that is, one outside consecrated ground, with a stake driven through the heart, and the body buried without ceremony at a crossroads. (This was done in order to prevent the spirit finding its way home to haunt any former associates.) The spot chosen for the interment was the junction of Cannon Street Road and Cable Street – immediately adjacent to where, just a few weeks previously, the Marr family had been buried in the shadow of Nicholas Hawksmoor's great church of St George's in the East.

FRANZ MÜLLER,
BRITAIN'S FIRST EVER TRAIN MURDERER (1864)

STRANGE THINGS GET LEFT ON TRAINS: in 1919 Colonel T. E. Lawrence ('of Arabia') mislaid his quarter-of-a-million-word memoir and was forced to rewrite the entire thing. Every year, in fact, Transport for London's lost property department deals with such losses, finding more than 160,000 misplaced items, from outboard motors and 14' canoes to multiple glass eyes, a box of stuffed bats, countless inflatable dolls and even a bag containing two human skulls.

But arguably the most significant item ever left behind was a distinctive gentleman's black beaver hat, discovered on 9 July 1864 in a compartment of a North London Railway train running an evening service between Fenchurch Street and Hackney Wick.

The carriage had recently been vacated by an elderly bank official named Thomas Briggs, a resident of Clapton Square. He was found badly injured by the side of the track after the driver of another train reported seeing something suspicious on the stretch between Bow and Hackney Wick. Carried up the embankment and into a local pub called the Mitford Castle, the old man subsequently died of his injuries, thereby earning the dubious honour of being the first person in this country to be murdered on a train.

– and, curiously, his eye-glasses – and had then been beaten up and heaved out of the window of the moving train. His assailant had left the train before it made its return journey to the City, during which two commuters discovered a pool of blood on the floor of the carriage – together with the aforementioned hat.

Prior to the killing the public had shown itself still to be generally unsure about these new-fangled railways. Things had got off to a shaky start when MP William Huskisson had been mown down and killed by Stephenson's *Rocket*, and more than 30 years later many Londoners still imagined that trains were simply too fast and that passengers risked suffocating if they travelled at speed. A brutal murder was the last thing the heavily indebted railway companies needed, and soon a mammoth £300 reward was being offered for any information leading to an arrest.

Alarmed at this, the hat's owner – a 25-year-old German gunsmith called Franz Müller, who had been working in the area as a tailor – headed for the United States. But the police were hot on his tail: publicity about the murder had prompted a jeweller in Cheapside to come forward, claiming that, two days after the murder, he had been offered a gold chain by a man with a German accent. Shortly afterwards a cabbie provided a photograph of Müller, a friend of his daughter's, whom the jeweller was able to identify as the same man. After Müller had been traced to an address in what is now Old Ford Road, Bethnal Green, a warrant was quickly issued for his arrest when a neighbour confirmed that he had boarded a ship for America.

Two Scotland Yard detectives travelled to Liverpool and boarded a fast steamship in the hope that they could meet Müller when he stepped ashore in New York. Luck and technology were on their side – Müller was travelling more slowly, by sail – and the hapless German was arrested as he stepped onto the gangplank. He was wearing a hat later identified as belonging to Thomas Briggs, thereby explaining why his own had been found on the train. During the crossing he had customised it slightly, using his skills as a tailor to lower the crown to produce a more fashionable profile.

There is still some confusion as to whether Müller was fleeing the crime or had committed the crime in order to pay his passage, but either way he had Briggs's hat and gold fob watch in his possession and was charged with murder. After a short trial back in London, and with the public clamouring for revenge, he was found guilty and sentenced to hang.

Executions at this time were still carried out in public, and with the best seats selling for the equivalent of 10 times a labourer's weekly wage, the crowd that gathered outside Newgate Gaol on 14 November 1864 was immense. Local pubs were doing a roaring trade and the friendly atmosphere soon turned riotous, leading to scenes that contributed to the decision, four years later, to conduct all future executions within the prison walls. At the same time it was decreed that railway companies should install some means of communication between individual carriages and the guard, and a millinery craze started for a style now rechristened 'the Müller Cut-down'.

HENRY WAINWRIGHT OR PERCY KING?
THE DANGERS OF A DOUBLE LIFE (1874)

- VINE COURT, E1
- 40 TREDEGAR SQUARE, E1

LIVING TWO LIVES SIMULTANEOUSLY, and at two separate addresses, 36-year-old Henry Wainwright was a successful commercial brush manufacturer, a respectable teetotal churchwarden living in tasteful comfort at 40 Tredegar Square, and by all accounts a good father to his children. Unfortunately for them Wainwright was also a serial philanderer who, just a mile and a half away, had fathered two little girls with a woman who knew him as Percy King. He was not technically a bigamist, however, because although 'Mrs King' liked to be known as such the two merely cohabited. She was in reality a hatmaker's assistant called Harriet Lane.

On 11 September 1875 Miss Lane was pronounced dead, the precise nature of her injuries obscured by the fact that she was found cut up into 10 pieces and bundled into a couple of hastily wrapped parcels that had been buried – a year earlier – beneath what is now Vine Court but at the time was the yard of Wainwright's warehouse at 215 Whitechapel Road. Now renumbered 130, his business was conveniently located approximately halfway between his two otherwise unconnected lives.

TREDEGAR SQUARE

VINE COURT

is extraordinary double life, and indeed Harriet's murder, only came to light when Wainwright was compelled to surrender the lease due to financial troubles.

When the four-wheeled cab, or 'growler', he had hired arrived at the warehouse to remove his belongings, one of the men working there was told to carry two foul-smelling parcels out to it. Poking around in one of them, and finding what was clearly a human hand, the employee nevertheless did as he was told – but decided to follow the cab at a safe distance once his employer had climbed aboard.

WAINWRIGHT WAS FOR A SERIAL KILLER A MISFIT

Keeping out of sight he followed the cab over London Bridge and all the way to an address near the Hop Exchange in Borough: only then was he able to alert a police constable to what he had found. Given that he was riding in the cab, it was inevitable that the bearded, respectable and comfortably bourgeois Wainwright should come under immediate suspicion, but his arrest must have proved profoundly shocking to his legitimate family and to those who moved in the same circles.

It was soon revealed that the same money worries that had forced Wainwright's move from the warehouse had also put pressure on his relationship with Harriet. Some months previously he had moved her and the two girls into cheaper accommodation, and reduced her allowance. Harriet had taken great exception to this and, something of a drinker, voiced her objections so forcefully that 'Percy' decided enough was enough. After preparing a shallow grave behind the warehouse and procuring a gun, Wainwright persuaded Harriet to visit the premises. On arrival she was shot in the head, had her throat slit for good measure, and was then buried in the pit beneath a layer of disinfecting chloride of lime. With his brother's help, Wainwright concocted a story to cover her sudden disappearance, making it look as though Harriet was planning a trip to Paris with a purely fictional 'Mr Frieake'.

Incredibly, once in court, Wainwright insisted that he had no idea what the parcels contained, and that for a cash sum from a complete stranger he had simply agreed to store them for a while and later to transport them across the river. But the gun was shown to be his, he had been caught actually in possession of the remains of his former lover, and there was even a suggestion that he had attempted to bribe the policeman in Southwark rather than hand over the parcels. Found guilty of the murder of Harriet Louisa Lane on what the judge called 'the clearest and most convincing evidence', Henry Wainwright was sentenced to be hanged on 21 December 1875 at Newgate Gaol.

The decision, less than a decade earlier, to stop executing criminals in public – the last in London had been that of the Fenian Michael Barrett on 26 May 1868 – might have led Wainwright to expect a dignified and private demise. This was not to be, however, and the following day *The Times* was one of many to describe in detail the instrument of execution – 'peculiar in construction and appearance; it being roofed over, lighted with lamps at each end, and having a deep pit, over which a chain and noose were suspended' – as well as listing by name and rank the scores of City dignitaries who had shouldered their way into the yard at Newgate to see justice done. The execution of this seemingly upstanding family man had become the must-see event of the year.

JACK THE RIPPER –
THE QUINTESSENTIAL
LONDON MURDERER (1888)

- **DURWARD STREET, E1**
- **MITRE SQUARE, EC3**
- **GUNTHORPE STREET, E1**

BY FAR THE MOST DOCUMENTED yet still the most mysterious of the capital's killers, Jack was active for only a few months – and his tally of five victims awful but relatively modest.

But no other serial killer to date has exercised quite such a hold on the British imagination or garnered quite so many theories as to who was responsible and how, precisely, he, she or they got away with it. An internet search for the Ripper throws up literally millions of pages; new books, films, theories and even computer games on the subject are launched with metronomic regularity; organised Jack the Ripper walks take place every week of the year in East London; and nearly half a century after the last body was found, a successful wigmaker in Wardour Street was still advertising his business by claiming to have unwittingly provided Jack's disguise all those years earlier.

The guided walks are incredibly popular, too, and this despite the fact that, while we know the names of the victims – Mary Ann Nichols, Annie Chapman, Elizabeth Stride, Catherine Eddowes and Mary Jane Kelly – the crime scenes have all but one disappeared in the process of building,

DURWARD STREET

MITRE SQUARE

GUNTHORPE STREET

bombing, burning and rebuilding over the last century. Running off the High Street in Whitechapel, one side of Gunthorpe Street, with its arched entrance and cobbled surface, still gives a fair impression of late-1880s London, however, and indeed the murder here of Martha Tabram on 7 August 1888 – in what was then called George Yard – has occasionally been added to Jack's tally.

Most research suggests we can only be sure of the first five named above, however, and of these the location of Mary Ann's killing three weeks after Martha Tabram's is the only one still to bear much resemblance to its likely appearance on 31 August 1888. Back then Durward Street was called Buck's Row – it was renamed because of the murder – and what was then the Board School is now apartments, but the small yard where the 41-year-old prostitute's body was discovered in the early hours by a cart driver has survived more or less intact.

The same cannot be said for 29 Hanbury Street, a slum torn down in 1960s, but this was where the disembowelled body of Annie Chapman was found by one of 17 residents on 8 September. No-one had heard a thing in the night and this second death ignited a panic in the area, talk of the 'Whitechapel Murders' reaching fever pitch on the 30th with the discovery of a third mutilated body. Elizabeth Stride's corpse was found on the site of what is now Harry Gosling Primary School in Henriques Street (Berner Street at the time) on the other side of the Commercial Road.

Less than an hour later another gruesome discovery, this one within the historic City boundary, took Jack's total to four. The body of Catherine Eddowes was found in Mitre Square – a colourful flower bed now marks the spot – as a result of which scores of City of London police joined the hunt. It was perhaps because of this that Jack appeared to have taken the decision to lay low for a while.

On 9 November the fifth and final murder was perpetrated not far away in a room in Miller's Court, the only Ripper crime scene to be photographed. Perhaps the worst attack of all, Mary Jane Kelly's mutilation was so complete as to render her corpse unrecognisable. The room itself – now lost beneath the City Corporation's multi-storey car park on White's Row – was so soaked in blood and gore that her landlord described the carnage as 'more like the work of a devil than the work of a man'.

THE KILLINGS STOPPED AS SUDDENLY AS THEY HAD STARTED

Adding to the mystique that already surrounded the case, the killings then stopped as suddenly as they had started. Police continued to find clues chalked up on the walls around Whitechapel – as many hoaxes as not, and often implicating local Jews or Freemasons – and another two murders were subsequently attributed to Jack, although both have since been discounted.

Thereafter the Ripper's only victim seemed to be the Metropolitan Commissioner, Sir Charles Warren, whose inability to find the killer led to him being forced out of office by public opinion. But there were, in a sense, other victims: the many men who were rumoured at the time to be Jack but had no opportunity to clear their names. These include Seweryn Antonowicz Klosowski (see p.192), Thomas Neill Cream (p.188) and even Walter Sickert (p.161), all of whose names keep popping into the frame but without a shred of anything one might realistically term evidence.

'PETER THE PAINTER',
THE HOUNDSDITCH MURDERS AND THE SIEGE OF SIDNEY STREET (1910)

CUTLER STREET, E1
SIDNEY STREET, E1

ON 16 DECEMBER 1910, City of London police were called after neighbours heard what sounded like thieves breaking in to a jeweller's shop on Houndsditch by tunnelling into the shop from the Exchange Buildings to the rear. Nine policemen, some uniformed and others in plain clothes, responded to the call-out, three of whom were fatally wounded (and another two injured) when they knocked on the door and attempted to enter.

Clearly the police had expected nowhere near this level of resistance, assuming that they were simply interrupting a burglary, but in fact the two gunmen and up to eight accomplices were members of the Latvian anarchist group Liesma, or the Gardstein Gang. Desperately needing to raise funds for their political struggle against Russian rule, they had alighted on the shop of H. S. Harris in the mistaken belief that the vault contained items belonging to the Tsar.

Following what is still the bloodiest single-day assault on serving British police officers, the gang attempted to escape through the back of the premises. They emerged onto Cutler Street, carrying one of their number whom they had shot by mistake and who subsequently died once they had holed up at 59 Grove Road in Mile End. Amid rumours that the gang was led by a notorious revolutionary known only as

Near to this spot on the 16 December 1910
three City of London Police Officers were
fatally wounded preventing a robbery at
119 Houndsditch

In commemoration of
Sgt Robert Bentley
Sgt Charles Tucker
PC Walter C. Choat

Where courage and sense of duty will not be forgotten

CUTLER STREET

SIDNEY STREET

'Peter the Painter', the police mounted a search of the area, which continued over several weeks.

A lucky break came on 3 January, when a tip-off led police to another house, 100 Sidney Street, in which two or three gang members were said to be hiding. One might have assumed the authorities would take no chances this time, but once again an unarmed officer was sent to knock on the door – and once again he was answered by a hail of bullets. The officer survived with no more than a punctured lung and an injured foot, but faced with an unknown number of assailants – and with the police inadequately armed with a variety of bulldog revolvers, shotguns and rifles fitted with .22 Morris-tube barrels – an order for reinforcements was sent to St John's Wood barracks.

With a detachment of Scots Guards soon in attendance – and later Home Secretary Winston Churchill, complete with top hat and cigar – what became known as the Siege of Sidney Street developed into a great public spectacle. Reporters crowded into the area to get the story, and local householders charged good money for a place on any rooftop with a reasonable view of the action.

Before long, soldiers, policemen and the gunmen were all trading fire, but the question of tactics – who should get the honour of storming the building – was put on hold when smoke began pouring from the windows. The fire brigade arrived but was told not to turn its hoses on, Churchill perhaps being keen to flush out the gunmen like rats at stubble-burning time. In the end he relented, to save neighbouring properties, but only after the roof and upper floors of no. 100 had collapsed.

Once the flames had died down and officers were able to enter the building, only two bodies came to light: Fritz Svaars and William Sokolow. There was no sign of the mysterious Peter, and the press lauded his ability to slip away unnoticed yet again. For months afterwards the newspapers speculated on the fate of this elusive character: that he had gone down with the *Lusitania* in 1915, or had resurfaced in Moscow to lead the 1917 Bolshevik Revolution. The likelihood is that Peter the Painter never existed, and that he was – much like the bullet rumoured to have creased Churchill's top hat that day – merely a press invention designed to enhance what was already quite a story.

Remarkably, given the size of the gang involved, no-one ever stood trial for the attempted burglary nor for the three murders that resulted from it. And while the police could be forgiven for walking into such an unexpected ambush, the subsequent siege taught them a useful lesson, namely that, as a force, they were woefully ill-equipped to deal with a new generation of well-armed and dangerously effective criminals.

In 2010, to mark the 100th anniversary of their deaths, a plaque in commemoration of Sergeants Robert Bentley and Charles Tucker and PC Walter Choat was unveiled on a wall in Cutler Street, near where the jewellery shop once stood. More curiously, four years earlier, a block of flats on Sidney Street had officially been named Painter House after the elusive Peter – described on its commemorative plaque as an 'antihero' rather than a terrorist, armed robber and murderer – while the neighbouring block was named Siege House.

THE KRAY TWINS'
DREAM OF A PERFECT
CRIME (1966)

THE BLIND BEGGAR, 337 WHITECHAPEL ROAD, E1

STEP ACROSS MILE END ROAD from Sidney Street and it is hard to miss the
Blind Beggar, a large and distinctive Victorian gin palace built in 1894 on
the site of the old Mile End tollgate. As infamous these days as Rillington
Place, this is the pub in which, on 9 March 1966, Ronnie Kray casually
shot dead a rival gang member called George Cornell.

It would be another two years before Kray was arrested and sent down
for this murder, and the papers the next morning made no mention of
gang warfare, observing merely that the 38-year-old Cornell ('also known
as Myers') hailed from Camberwell and had died on the operating table
after being shot in the head. Nor was any particular connection made with
the Blind Beggar, scene of another murder some years previously, when a
man had been stabbed in the eye with a brolly. Several witnesses had seen
the shooting and were able to confirm what Cornell was drinking (a G&T)
and even the record that was playing on the jukebox at the time ('The Sun
Ain't Gonna Shine Anymore' by the Walker Brothers), but no-one could
or wished to identify Ronnie Kray, who strolled out of the pub and into
a waiting car.

When Ronnie and his brother Reggie were eventually arrested on
8 May 1968, Cornell's murder was just one of the crimes of which they

stood accused. For years, brief periods under arrest and incarceration had been punctuated by a series of criminal acts encompassing everything from arson to fraud, racketeering to hijacking, armed robbery to at least one other murder. (Lured to his death at Evering Road, Stoke Newington, in October 1967, Jack 'The Hat' McVitie had been repeatedly stabbed by Reggie, keen to demonstrate that he was his brother's equal.) The twins had also engaged in a long-running battle with their South London rivals the Richardsons, whose associates included George Cornell.

'AND THERE IN COLD BLOOD SLAY ANOTHER HUMAN BEING'

Since starting out in the 1950s, Ronnie, who suffered from paranoid schizophrenia, is said to have dreamed of committing the perfect crime, which for him was a Chicago-gangster-style hit of the sort he attempted to pull off at the Blind Beggar: calm, audacious, unhurried, and – if only to those who inexplicably still hold a candle for the Krays – infinitely cool. Cornell's death was meant to demonstrate the twins' rise above mere criminality, and their supposed supremacy over rival 'business' concerns. Counting showbiz faces and political figures among their friends, famously photographed by David Bailey and interviewed on television, the Krays' loss of perspective is perhaps understandable but no less risible for that. In court things were quickly put back into context, however, Kenneth Jones QC for the prosecution condemning the 'horrifying effrontery, the deadly effrontery of two men who can walk into a public house in this land of ours on any evening and there in cold blood slay another human being'.

In order for their reign of terror to succeed, the twins, still in their mid-30s at the time of their arrest, had relied on their ability to silence any opposition, to rule their streets through fear. But once the police finally went for them – Inspector Leonard 'Nipper' Read was allowed a team of 27 to build a case – they found themselves on remand, whereupon witnesses slowly came forward and were persuaded to talk.

Ronnie may have been smart enough to leave no forensic evidence when he sauntered out of the Blind Beggar, but in court his getaway driver turned Queen's Evidence and identified Cornell's assailant by pointing out Ronnie Kray and referring to 'the fat one with the glasses'. Another witness was able to testify that a total of three shots had been fired, one finding its mark on Cornell's forehead. As the victim lay dying on the floor of the pub, the court heard, two men who had been drinking with him took to their heels, two more customers ducked out of sight, and the barmaid disappeared down into the cellar. In court she was identified only as 'Mrs X', a witness for the prosecution, and she admitted that she had not come forward earlier for fear that 'Ronnie would have shot me'.

Retiring for very nearly seven hours after an exhausting 39-day trial, the jury found Mrs X's evidence compelling and dismissed the twins' appeals of innocence. Sentencing both to life imprisonment, Mr Justice Melford Stevenson patiently explained to the twins that, 'In my view, society has earned a rest from your activities.'

A RARE MURDER
ON THE UNDERGROUND (1976)

✹ WEST HAM STATION, E15

WITH ELEVEN LINES, more than 250 miles of track, 269 stations and an incredible 1 billion passengers per year, the Tube is among the world's most extensive underground railways, as well as being the oldest. Given all this, it is inevitable that the Tube could never have remained a crime-free zone, although most of the offences committed on the network are relatively minor, with approximately 550 thefts reported each year and some 200 incidents involving knives.

With the notable exception of large-scale terror outrages like the 7/7 attacks, deaths are still commendably rare. Of those that do occur the vast majority are suicides, happening at a rate of approximately one a week, which is equivalent to the combined totals of the Paris Metro and the New York Subway. (The most popular time for jumping is 11am, and the most popular stations are Kings Cross and Victoria.) Among the better-known victims are musicians Graham Bond at Finsbury Park in 1974 (the eponymous Organisation's mellotron man) and The Sound's Adrian Borland, who threw himself under a train at Wimbledon in 1999. Technically both were committing a criminal offence, and, had they survived, could have been charged with endangering safety on the railway and the obstruction of a train with intent.

A couple of years before Borland's death the *Independent* ran a story concerning a worrying escalation in violence underground – after eight

women had been held up at gunpoint – but murders are still sufficiently rare to make each one noteworthy. Back in 1914, the body of seven-year-old Margaret Nally had been found in the ladies' cloakroom at Aldersgate Street station (now Barbican). She had been sexually assaulted and then suffocated using a piece of fabric pushed down her throat. Then, in 1957, Countess Teresa Lubienska, a Polish aristocrat, wartime resistance fighter and concentration camp survivor, was stabbed to death at Gloucester Road. On neither occasion was the murderer apprehended or identified.

The third death occurred on 15 March 1976, when 34-year-old Julius Stephen, a West Indian Tube driver from Hammersmith, bravely pursued an IRA gunman named Vincent Kelly, who had detonated a bomb on his train as it pulled away from West Ham station. It is thought the 5lb bomb was intended to cause rush-hour panic at Liverpool Street station, but that the terrorist unwittingly got on a train heading the wrong way along what was then the Metropolitan Line.

Nine people were injured in the blast, and both Stephen and a 24-year-old Post Office engineer named Peter Chalk were shot when they gave chase. Stephen died instantly, leaving a wife and young son.

This was the third such incident in recent weeks, but the only one to prove fatal. On 13 February a much larger bomb had been defused at Oxford Circus, and on 4 March a 10lb device exploded in a carriage outside Cannon Street. Fortunately on this last occasion the train was empty, but eight passengers were injured on a train coming the other way. Shortly afterwards, armed plain-clothes policemen started patrolling the stations. Other IRA attacks over the period were to prove yet more devastating and continued against even softer targets such as Harrods, a bandstand in Regent's Park and a ceremonial detachment of guardsmen from the Household Cavalry. The results were frequently horrendous, although London and Londoners proved their resilience again and again, and not for the last time the capital refused to be brought to its knees by terrorist gangs.

Having shot and killed Stephen, Vincent Kelly was chased by police and he turned his gun on himself when he was cornered. Using the usual circumlocutions, the BBC subsequently reported that 'armed detectives are currently guarding a man at Queen Mary's Hospital, West Ham', the suspect described as being in his mid-thirties with an Irish accent and a London address. Investigations subsequently revealed that Kelly had boarded an outward-bound train at Stepney Green, realised his mistake when the train surfaced at Plaistow and then swapped onto a train heading back into the centre. The mistake had badly upset his schedule, but he was merely injured rather than incapacitated by his own blast and was able to escape through the driver's cab.

At the Old Bailey in 1977, Kelly received five life sentences – for bombing a London Underground train, killing the driver, and the attempted murder of another man – but was subsequently released as part of the 1998 Good Friday Agreement.

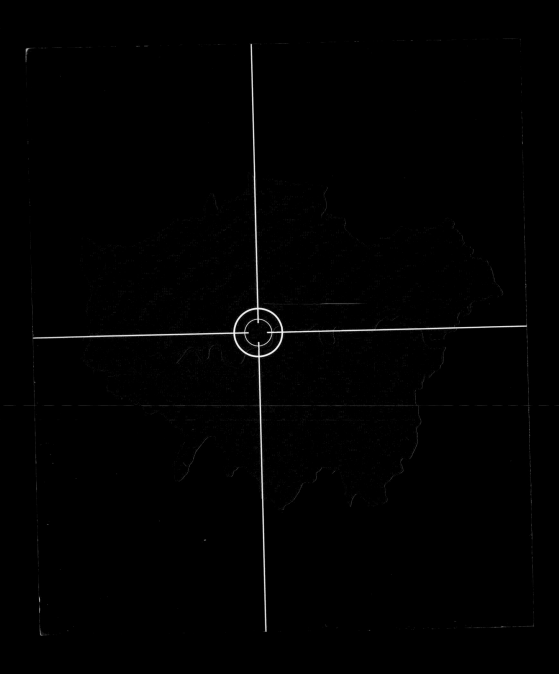

WEST END 2

MURDERS OF LONDON

THE **IRA** TARGETS
SIR HENRY WILSON
(1922)

- **36 EATON PLACE, SW1**
- **LIVERPOOL STREET WAR MEMORIAL, EC3**

FIELD MARSHAL SIR HENRY HUGHES WILSON, BT. GCB DSO MP remains the archetype of a certain class of public servant, born in Ireland and educated in England before embarking on an impressive military career serving the Empire. After failing repeatedly to win a place at either the Royal Military Academy at Woolwich or the junior establishment at Sandhurst, Wilson joined a local militia before transferring in the 1880s to the more prestigious Rifle Brigade. Service overseas followed, principally in Burma and India, but an injury left him walking with a stick for the remainder of his life. Returned to Britain, he worked in intelligence at the War Office before being given the command of a battalion in his old brigade and later at Sandhurst.

Wilson's advancement during the Great War was equally impressive, Winston Churchill (at this time at the Admiralty) recognising that, in him, 'the War Cabinet found for the first time an expert adviser of superior intellect.' An enthusiast for a new species of armoured vehicles that was gradually supplanting the mounted horse, Churchill was no doubt delighted by Wilson's decision to more than double the size of the Tank Regiment. Having been made a baronet and awarded £10,000 and the

EATON PLACE

LIVERPOOL STREET WAR MEMORIAL

rank of Field Marshal after the Armistice, Wilson decided next to exchange military life for politics. In 1922 he won a seat in Parliament and accepted a role as security adviser to the new Northern Ireland Government.

Unfortunately this brought Sir Henry into the sights of the London branch of the new Irish Republican Army, an organisation that had grown out of the Easter Uprising and the Irish Volunteers. The London faction firmly opposed the Anglo-Irish Treaty, which the previous year had created the Irish Free State. Numbered among its young firebrands were Joseph O'Sullivan and Reginald Dunne, two 24-year-olds who had previously served in the British Army. Discharged in 1917 on losing a leg at Ypres, O'Sullivan had been able to secure menial work at the Ministry of Munitions and may have been able to use his position in order to feed low-level intelligence back to his political masters. He was also implicated in the 1921 murder of Vincent Fovargue, an IRA informer who was found dead on a golf course near Staines with a label pinned to him reading: 'Let spies and traitors beware – IRA'.

In mid-June 1923 he and Dunne were informed that Sir Henry was due to unveil a new war memorial at Liverpool Street station. (This is still in situ, on a raised walkway adjacent to a branch of McDonald's.) The two men waited for him to return to his home in Eaton Place, whereupon he was shot three times and killed on the doorstep. A crowd quickly formed, and in attempting to escape the Irishmen fired several times, injuring two policemen and a member of the public.

With just the one leg O'Sullivan made it only as far as Ebury Street before he was captured, as was Dunne when he turned back in a bid to help his friend. Their weapons were quickly conveyed to the Cabinet Office at no. 10, where Churchill and Prime Minister Lloyd George stood on either side of the room's famous table silently contemplating the pistols that been used to take their colleague's life. Sir Henry's political career had been exceptionally short – his maiden speech to the House of Commons had been made just three months previously – but business in the chamber was adjourned immediately, and at Buckingham Palace a birthday banquet for the Prince of Wales was cancelled.

The two assassins refused to reveal their identities or occupations, but the following day the *Belfast Telegraph*, among others, named them as James Connolly and John O'Brien. On 10 August, after a short trial, they were hanged. A plaque was subsequently affixed to the aforementioned war memorial, recording the murder of Sir Henry within two hours of the official unveiling ceremony.

'THE FOULEST IN THE FOUL CATEGORY OF IRISH POLITICAL CRIMES'

Although Sir Henry was in some regards a logical target for such an outrage, Connolly and O'Brien's precise motive has never been explained. As the IRA was at this time deeply divided over whether or not to support the 1921 Treaty, it has been suggested that the assassination was intended to provoke the British into declaring war on Eire – thereby bringing the two sides of the Republican movement together. In this respect, at least, what *The Times* described as 'among the foulest in the foul category of Irish political crimes' must be judged to have failed.

ELVIRA BARNEY'S
DEADLY LOVER'S
TIFF (1932)

THE YOUNG SOCIALITE DAUGHTER of Sir John and Lady Mullen, Elvira Barney was separated from her musician husband and living the life in a tiny Knightsbridge mews house. In the early hours of 31 May 1932, the 27-year-old rang her doctor and asked him to come over. Told only that there had been 'a terrible accident', Dr Thomas Durrant arrived to find the body of Barney's lover Michael Scott Stephen at the foot of the stairs.

Visibly upset and very agitated, Barney was at great pains to tell the doctor that, as he lay dying, Stephen had been saying, over and over, 'Why doesn't the doctor come? I want to tell him it was not your fault.' The accident, if indeed that is what it was, had evidently involved a .32 Smith & Wesson revolver, clearly fired at very close range and now lying close to Stephen's body. A subsequent examination of the weapon revealed that two of its six chambers were empty.

Barney was arrested on suspicion of murder but told police that the gun had gone off accidentally during a struggle between the two of them. Stephen, she said, had threatened to kill himself with it. Neighbours in the narrow mews were able to confirm that the two had indeed been fighting – 'There was a terrible barney at no.21,' is how one of them put it – and that this was a far-from-rare occurrence. Apparently the couple had returned

home earlier in the evening from a party at the famous Café de Paris in Coventry Street, near Leicester Square. One of their fights had started soon afterwards, with Mrs Barney at one point being heard to scream, 'Get out! Get out of my house! I will shoot you! I will shoot you!' This had been followed by a loud bang – the sound of the revolver going off – after which she was heard saying, 'Chicken, chicken, come back to me. I will do anything you want me to.'

'THERE WAS A TERRIBLE BARNEY AT NO. 21'

A search of the premises revealed plenty of evidence of the couple's louche lifestyle, in particular what the journalist Macdonald Hastings later memorably described as 'a wall painting which would have been a sensation in a brothel in Pompeii. The library was furnished with publications which could never have passed through His Majesty's Customs.' The house was equipped with what he describes as 'implements of fetishism and perversion', and it was known that the pair's lifestyle had relied heavily on illegal stimulants.

On 3 June Barney was duly charged with Stephen's murder, but was allowed home to her parents' house at 6 Belgrave Square rather than being remanded in custody as might have been the case were she not so well connected. The trial, in which the society angle was bound to generate enormous public interest around the English-speaking world, began on 4 July. Barney was represented by none other than the Attorney General, Sir Patrick Hastings (no relation to Macdonald), whose intention was to prove that the gun had gone off accidentally, despite a witness for the prosecution testifying to at least one other occasion on which Barney had shot at her lover in the street. Sir Patrick took the opportunity to demonstrate to the jury how the lack of a safety catch and an exceptionally light trigger action made an accidental firing more likely than not, and, after a summing up that the judge described as the best he had ever witnessed, Mrs Barney stepped out of the dock and slunk back into society.

Unfortunately for her, the verdict proved, if anything, even more of a scandal than the revelations regarding her lifestyle. Initially the court of public opinion seemed satisfied, with crowds singing 'For she's a jolly good fellow' outside the court, and bouquet after bouquet arriving at Belgrave Square. But the mood gradually turned against her, particularly when a report appeared in the press suggesting that she had returned to the Café de Paris and, after a few too many, been heard to shout out, 'I am the one who shot her lover, so take a good look at me.'

Gradually press interest in Barney waned, however, and she moved to France. On Christmas Day 1936 it was reported that a Miss Elvira Mullen had been found dead in her Paris hotel room, having collapsed after what had clearly been a riotous tour of the cafés and bars of Montmartre and the Quartier Latin.

The London mews in which the alleged crime occurred has since been rebuilt, but the numbering has remained unchanged.

LEOPOLD VON HOESCH –
THE RELUCTANT NAZI (1936)

9 CARLTON HOUSE TERRACE, SW1

IN A TINY GARDEN AT THE TOP of the Duke of York Steps in St James's is a carefully tended Nazi-era memorial. It looks out over a number of more imposing reminders of the British Empire, including monuments to Edward VII, Scott of the Antarctic and Sir John Franklin, and even the Duke of Wellington, whose personal mounting block still stands outside the old United Service Club fronting onto Pall Mall.

Today the offending item is protected behind a sheet of glass, but it can still be read: Ein treuer Begleiter, 'a true companion'. The reference is to a German Shepherd dog named Giro, buried here in February 1934 after coming into contact with some exposed electrical wiring at the German Embassy next door. His master – Dr Leopold von Hoesch (1881–1936) – was at the time German ambassador to the Court of St James's, which presumably explains the rather privileged location of Giro's final resting place.

In 1934, with Hitler fast consolidating his grip on power, relations between Britain and Germany were cooling fast, although they had yet to become openly warlike. Von Hoesch was himself an unenthusiastic Nazi who, having played a significant role in normalising relations between the Great War powers and his own defeated nation, was regarded as a statesman of both skill and charm. A popular figure on the London scene, who could count as friends a number of senior British politicians,

his sudden death in 1936 was a potential blow to international relations. Because of this, and in line with normal protocols for an ambassador dying in office, von Hoesch was accorded what amounted to a state funeral before leaving London for the last time. This included a 19-gun salute, a detachment of Grenadier Guards marching alongside Nazi troops accompanying the ceremonial gun limber on which his swastika-draped coffin was borne to Victoria Station, and a phalanx of British cabinet ministers on hand to lead the mourners.

Officially von Hoesch had died of a stroke, which was unusual but by no means unprecedented for a man in his mid-50s. But the arrival of his replacement – the reviled Joachim von Ribbentrop, who caused a scandal by greeting King George VI with a straight-armed Sieg heil – raised suspicions in both political and social circles that Giro's master had deliberately been bumped off. Never a supporter of von Ribbentrop and dismissive of his erratic behaviour and arrogant and tactless methods, von Hoesch had frequently criticised him in diplomatic dispatches. He would doubtless have agreed with an assessment made 60 years later by the historian Lawrence Rees – which labelled von Ribbentrop 'the Nazi almost all the other Nazis hated' – but unfortunately, with Hitler in power, it was very much von Ribbentrop's star that was in the ascendency rather than von Hoesch's.

The latter's patriotism was never in doubt, but neither was his antipathy towards the extremes of Nazism; discharging what he saw as his responsibilities as ambassador on a number of occasions brought him into dangerous conflict with his increasingly powerful rival. For example, memoranda drafted by von Hoesch and transmitted to Berlin correctly warned that the opinions of some of von Ribbentrop's most prized contacts – which included George Bernard Shaw, Sir Austen Chamberlain and the marquesses of Lothian and Londonderry – could no longer be regarded as representative of the true direction or strength of British feelings towards Germany. At the same time, his claim that German remilitarisation of the Rhineland in March 1936 would inflame French and British opinion, making another war more not less likely, was bound to infuriate the Führer, for whom it was a vital strategic move (and one he had argued for in the pages of *Mein Kampf*).

Given all this, it is arguable that von Hoesch could not have been allowed to remain in post, and certainly his timely death avoided any diplomatic complications that might have resulted from his being recalled. His murder would have been neither difficult to arrange nor to cover up, British authorities having no right to examine a body within a foreign embassy. The cover story of a stroke or heart attack would also have saved his family from dishonour, or further persecution by the Nazis.

As a footnote, it is curious to note that, despite the considerable damage suffered by many buildings and memorials in the surrounding area at the hands of Luftwaffe, and despite the natural antipathy towards Germany at this time, Giro's grave somehow came through the war unscathed. A stroke of good fortune – but also, perhaps, an unusual tribute to Britain's well-advertised love of dogs.

BELATED – AND BLOODY – REVENGE FOR AMRITSAR (1940)

LIEUTENANT GOVERNOR OF THE PUNJAB during Lord Chelmsford's viceroyalty, Sir Michael O'Dwyer is best remembered for having supported the 1919 massacre of up to 1,000 unarmed Indian subjects at Amritsar, with many more than that number injured. His published description of the action as 'correct' rebounded on him more than 20 years later when he was shot dead inside what is now an unusually ornate Victorian apartment block close to New Scotland Yard.

The building was once Caxton Hall (now apartments) but for decades the registry office of choice for celebrity marriages including those of Peter Sellers, Elizabeth Taylor, Ingrid Bergman, Yehudi Menuhin, Ringo Starr and Mick Jagger. Its proximity to Westminster meant it was also an important gathering and rallying place for protest and lobby groups such as the Suffragettes.

On 13 March 1940 Sir Michael was booked to address a conference held here under the auspices of the East India Association and the Royal Central Asian Society. He also unexpectedly met his nemesis, a fanatical but patient supporter of the Indian independence movement called Shaheed Udham Singh.

The aforementioned massacre in the gardens of Jallianwala Bagh on 13 April 1919 had proved a turning point in Singh's life, an event he

witnessed personally when thousands of protesters were confronted by a small detachment of British troops under Brigadier General Reginald Dyer. Dyer's troops numbered fewer than 100, but equipped with the latest model of Enfield rifle they opened fire and continued to fire until their ammunition was exhausted. Throughout, Dyer ordered his men to fire low, which is to say not over the protesters' heads, also deliberately directing the fusillade to those places where the crowd was thickest. Witnesses later asserted that much of the fire had been concentrated on the exits from the gardens, thereby preventing anyone escaping what quickly became a hail of death.

The Indian National Conference subsequently claimed 1,000 dead and 1,500 injured, figures the official British report rejected in favour of 379 dead and 1,100 injured. But even these were considered too shocking for home consumption and suppressed, together with a cable to Dyer from O'Dwyer congratulating him on preventing a revolution. Unfortunately for both men, an official Committee of Enquiry found no evidence of such a revolution, and described as grave a number of errors, such as the lack of warning given and the duration of fire. O'Dwyer nevertheless stuck to his guns and in his memoirs insisted that, following this punishment, 'the Punjabis were quick to take to heart the lessons that revolution is a dangerous thing.'

This was clearly very far from the truth, however, in that the events of that day did nothing to slow demands in India for independence. Back home, Dyer was rewarded with a cash bounty by readers of one singularly pro-Empire British paper, the *Morning Post*. But he was branded the 'Butcher of Amritsar' by his many critics, with members on both sides of the House of Commons expressing their regret and revulsion at what had occurred.

Back in India, the national pain and humiliation proved too much to bear for one witness in particular. After visiting the nearby Harmandir Sahib (or Golden Temple), Udham Singh made a vow to join the struggle for Punjabi and Indian independence and to take revenge on those he felt were responsible. With a spell in jail for possession of unlicensed weapons and ammunition, it was a decade and a half before he was able to reach London. He moved into 9 Adler Street, between the Whitechapel and Commercial roads, and later to an address in Mornington Crescent. Having managed to buy a .45-calibre revolver and some ill-matched rounds from a soldier in a pub, he decided to bide his time and wait for an occasion when he could kill O'Dwyer with maximum impact.

'I DID IT BECAUSE I HAD A GRUDGE AGAINST HIM. HE DESERVED IT.'

The Caxton Hall meeting provided him with the perfect opportunity, and with the gun hidden in a book he had specially hollowed out for the purpose, Singh waited until the end of the meeting before opening fire. Killing his quarry and injuring the Indian Secretary of State and two others, he made no attempt at escape, instead admitting that he had done it, 'because I had a grudge against him. He deserved it. I don't belong to any society or anything else. I don't care, I don't mind dying.'

Requesting only that his remains be returned to the Punjab – a request that was denied for another 34 years – Shaheed Udham Singh refused to plead in court and was hanged at Pentonville on 31 July 1940.

'NOT SO 'LUCKY' LUCAN (1974)

- **46 LOWER BELGRAVE STREET, SW1**
- **PLUMBER'S ARMS, LOWER BELGRAVE STREET, SW1**

WHEN THE COUNTESS OF LUCAN rushed into a popular Belgravia pub on 7 November 1974 shouting 'Murder! There's been a murder!', she was dressed in nightclothes and bleeding heavily from a head wound. The phrase sparked a national manhunt, and launched one of the most extraordinary narratives of any twentieth-century English killer.

The focus of police enquiries was and remains her estranged husband, the 7th Earl, Richard John Bingham. At that time the Old Etonian lived a few minutes' walk away at 72a Elizabeth Street. A committed but largely unsuccessful gambler – despite his nickname, 'Lucky', the family silver was long gone – he had apparently let himself into the family home in Lower Belgrave Street and, some time after 9pm, attacked the children's new nanny, Mrs Sandra Rivett. The 39-year-old peer is widely assumed to have been after his wife, whom he blamed for the break-up of his marriage, the loss of custody of his children, and possibly somehow even his rising gambling debts. But having caught her husband literally red-handed and herself been roundly attacked, the Countess managed to escape and raise the alarm.

Rather than some splendid Palladian pile set among rolling acres, no.46 was a smart but discreet terraced house, typical of this part of the Duke of Westminster's London estate but by no means one of the large

PLUMBER'S ARMS

LOWER BELGRAVE STREET

cloistered clubland existence he had hitherto enjoyed.

In any event, and while the lack of a body means no death certificate can be issued, he has long since been declared dead. On 11 December 1992 Lucan was 'presumed deceased in chambers'; on 11 August 1999, a grant issued by the High Court of Justice stated unequivocally: 'BE IT KNOWN that the Right Honourable RICHARD JOHN BINGHAM 7th Earl of Lucan of 72a Elizabeth Street London SW1 died on or since the 8th day of November 1974.'

What is known is that the Ford Corsair he had been driving that night was found at Newhaven with its upholstery blood-stained, and that a length of lead piping found wrapped in surgical tape in the boot matched the one found in Lower Belgrave Street. Lucan's disappearance already looked highly suspicious, but this grisly discovery was enough for the police to issue an arrest warrant immediately. Interestingly it was also enough to have his lordship pronounced guilty, albeit not at the Old Bailey after a conventional trial by jury but in the Coroner's Court. An inquest held in June 1975 unanimously named the 7th Earl as the murderer of Mrs Rivett, the very last occasion on which this was allowed to happen: an inquest's right to name an individual as a murderer was shortly afterwards abolished by the Criminal Law Act (1977).

That said, and despite Lucan's presumed guilt in both the courts and public imagination, a number of unanswered questions continue to keep the mystery alive. Lucan was clearly a troubled individual under mounting pressure, and his behaviour was increasingly erratic. But few who knew him personally seemed to have thought him capable of murder, or considered him impulsive enough to launch such a violent and bloody attack without considering the consequences. It seems clear that he had made no real plans for an escape, but for many this just makes his successful disappearing act all the more impressive. For others it simply suggests that, having dumped the car at Newhaven and realised the game was up, the hapless peer probably jumped off a ferry and drowned.

LITVNENKO'S
KILLER COFFEE (2006)

- MILLENNIUM HOTEL, 44 GROSVENOR SQUARE, W1
- ITSU, 167 PICCADILLY, W1

IN NOVEMBER 2006 LONDON WAS THE SETTING for a murder straight
from the pages of an espionage novel, when traces of a deadly radioactive
isotope were found at a smart West End hotel and a branch of a well-known
sushi chain shortly after the death of a Russian dissident and former
KGB agent who had visited both premises.

The scare led to several hundred Londoners being tested for the effects
of radiation, but the real victim was Alexander Litvinenko. The 43-year-
old had fled Russia after working for 18 years at the KGB and its successor
organisation the FSB, having acquired a reputation since then as something
of a thorn in the side of the authorities in his home country. As the
Independent put it following his death at University College Hospital
on 23 November, Litvinenko 'occupied a world where intrigue, betrayal
and ruthless trickery were the tools of working life'. In that regard his
death should perhaps not have caused the media storm it did; as one
who lived by the sword, his untimely end might have been foreseen
with a certain inevitability.

The presumed presence of a foreign hitman in London was bound
to attract press interest, however, as indeed was the choice of weapon:
a hitherto little-known heavy metal called polonium-210. There were

MILLENNIUM HOTEL

ITSU, PICCADILLY

also plenty of rumours about the hit having been officially sanctioned rather than carried out by renegade agents or the so-called Russian mafia.

While it remains highly unlikely that such a thing will ever be proven, it was always clear that Litvinenko had done little to appease his enemies in Russia since claiming asylum in England in 2000. He had first come to prominence two years earlier after exposing an alleged plot to assassinate another erstwhile Kremlin insider, Boris Berezovsky, who had amassed a huge fortune before moving to Britain and spending quite a chunk of it on a large house in Surrey that had previously been owned by the DJ Chris Evans. Following this exposure Litvinenko had been arrested on charges of abusing his office by exceeding his authority, spending nine months in custody but eventually being acquitted.

His next brush with the law came with the publication of a book, *Blowing up Russia: Terror from Within*, in which he claimed that atrocities blamed on Chechen separatists were actually the work of the Russian Federal Security Service (FSB). Accusing its agents of killing more than 300 citizens this way, Litvinenko also alleged that the agency had been training Al-Qaeda no.2 Ayman al-Zawahiri in Dagestan before the events of 9/11.

By late 2006 Litvinenko had moved on to investigating the case of Anna Politkovskaya, a journalist whose enquiries into high-level corruption had been linked to her own murder in October that year. Just weeks after showing an interest in her death Litvinenko was himself taken ill, his physical decline so rapid that within days the keen runner was photographed in a hospital bed, bald, deathly pale, and unable to rise.

Still able at least to communicate effectively, Litvinenko described to police his recent movements. By tracking his progress from one appointment to another over the preceding couple of days, they discovered traces of the deadly radionuclide at several London addresses. These included Litvinenko's own home at 140 Osier Crescent in Muswell Hill and also several commercial premises; clearly aware of the methods employed by those active in the shadowy intelligence underworld, Litvinenko preferred to meet contacts at busy, public locations. A BBC timeline of his movements, including a meeting in Grosvenor Square with a former KGB colleague and a visit to the sushi bar on Piccadilly, reads like something from a John Le Carré novel, with the victim being admitted to one hospital and then transferred to another under heavy police guard. When his death was finally announced, the cause was put down first to a mysterious toxic substance but then to acute radiation poisoning, making Alexander Litvinenko the first ever victim of nuclear terrorism.

'INTRIGUE, BETRAYAL AND RUTHLESS TRICKERY WERE THE TOOLS OF WORKING LIFE'

The same BBC report also revealed that traces of radioactivity had been found at Heathrow – the Home Secretary John Reid confirming that two Russian aircraft were 'of interest' – but four days later, after British detectives had travelled to Moscow, the Russian Prosecutor General Yuri Chaika stated categorically that no one would be extradited to Britain in connection with the poisoning. Instead four diplomats were expelled from Britain, in response to which Russia made a similar gesture 72 hours later.

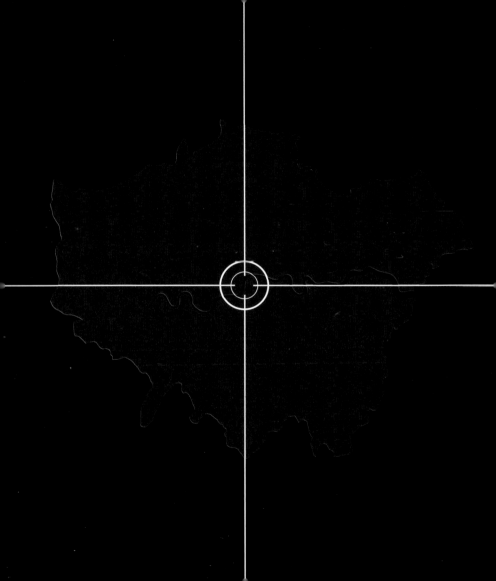

ON THE RIVER 3

MURDERS OF LONDON

WAS FREDDIE MILLS
JACK THE STRIPPER?
(1964)

WHILE THE PERPETRATOR has yet to be identified with any certainty, Londoners in the 1960s were gripped by a series of killings variously known as the Hammersmith Murders or Nude Murders, when six bodies were discovered along the West London stretch of the Thames over a period of just over a year.

The first victim, 30-year-old Hannah Tailford, was found dead near Hammersmith Bridge on 2 February 1964 with her underwear rammed down her throat. Like her, the subsequent victims were all working girls – two of them with a tangential connection to the previous year's Profumo Scandal – and all of them were strangled or choked while having sex. Their naked bodies were then dumped on waste ground or along the Thames shore by a mystery killer, whom the press promptly dubbed 'Jack the Stripper'. No-one was ever charged with any of the murders – or in connection with two superficially similar killings a few years earlier – although the name of boxer Freddie Mills came into the frame after his own death in July 1965.

Not long after the discovery of the last body, Mills had been found shot through the eye in his own car with a fairground rifle propped up between his legs. It was an unusual injury for a suicide, particularly as the eye is thought to have been open when the gun went off, but this was the official verdict. The car was parked in Goslett Yard off Charing Cross Road, close

to the Chinese restaurant in which the 1948 light-heavyweight world champion had invested much of his winnings from a successful career as a popular pugilist and fight promoter.

His death was always controversial, however, with family and friends (including several minor celebrities and some major criminals) insisting that suicide was just not in Freddie's make-up. Faced with this uncertainty the rumour mill ground into action to fill the vacuum, unsubstantiated claims quickly being made that Freddie, a family man, was up on an indecency charge in a public lavatory; that he had been bumped off by Chinese Triads wishing to move in on his Soho business interests; and that he had had an affair with Ronnie Kray.

THE CASE IS STILL
VERY FAR FROM CLOSED

But for now all this was still in the future. With the death count piling up along the Thames, the police launched a huge enquiry. After interviewing some 7,000 individuals, Scotland Yard announced that the number of suspects had been reduced to fewer than two dozen. Shortly afterwards this number was revised downwards to 10, and then to three, at which point the killings ceased as abruptly as they had begun. An observer might suggest that, seeing the odds of his being caught so dramatically shortened, the killer had sensibly decided to call it a day. The reality, however, is that serial killers are rarely able to control their urge to kill in this way; it is thought highly unlikely that such a prolific murderer could simply have melted into the background by returning to a more law-abiding lifestyle

Instead, the leading theory was that the killer had chosen to take his own life, and certainly a security guard working close to where the sixth girl was found came under suspicion after committing suicide. Subsequently it emerged that he was in Scotland at the time of at least one of the killings, which may explain why the Freddie Mills story came back into the frame.

It surfaced again most recently in 2001, in an *Observer* article. The story, headlined 'Boxing hero Freddie Mills "murdered eight women"', referred to a book entitled *South London Gangster*, in which Mills emerges as 'a vicious serial killer, responsible for the brutal deaths of at least eight young women whose naked bodies were found in or around the River Thames'. The book's author, Jimmy Tippett, interviewed several generations of East and South London 'faces', many known to him personally, and concluded that Mills, perhaps fearful that the police were closing in on him, decided to take his own life rather than risking the drop. By disguising it as a hit he may have hoped to save his family's feelings.

The case is still very far from closed, however, as other candidates have emerged in recent years, including a deceased detective chief superintendent (in Jimmy Evans and Martin Short's book *The Survivor*) and another writer with a particular interest in the subject, also now dead (in David Seabrook's *Jack of Jumps*). Nearly half a century on, the probability must be that we shall never know for sure.

LONDON'S NOTORIOUS
'UMBRELLA MURDER'
(1978)

WATERLOO BRIDGE, SE1

ON 7 SEPTEMBER 1978, while waiting at a bus stop at the southern end of Waterloo Bridge, broadcast journalist and Bulgarian dissident writer Georgi Ivanov Markov felt a momentary discomfort on the back of one leg. It was no worse than an insect sting, and he continued on his journey to work at the BBC World Service.

At first Markov assumed he had simply been accidentally jostled by the rush hour crowds – a pedestrian had even apologised for bumping into him – but four days later he was pronounced dead. Having developed a fever the first night, he alerted police to his suspicion that he had been poisoned – recalling, in particular, that after feeling the 'sting' he had noticed a man pick up an umbrella that had fallen to the ground and hurry off in the opposite direction. On arrival at the BBC he had found a small red pimple on the back of his right leg. The two, he felt sure, were not unconnected. A high-profile exile from Communism, and thus a definite candidate for the at-risk register, Markov had already received several death threats. Police were also aware that he ate only home-cooked meals, having been warned in an anonymous telephone call that he would eventually be poisoned. It was also noted that 7 September was the birthday of Todor Zhivkov, the Bulgarian leader.

Taking the dead man at his word, the police requested a detailed examination of the 49-year-old's body. Pathologists soon discovered a tiny spherical metal pellet embedded in Markov's calf. No larger than a pinhead, and made of an unusual platinum-iridium alloy, it had been hollowed out and still contained minute traces of a sugary compound together with some ricin, a poison for which there is no antidote. Experts at Porton Down, the top-secret government laboratory in Wiltshire, thought it likely that the sugary substance was used to seal the cavity. Carefully formulated to melt at precisely 37°C – human body temperature – it would then enable the release of the ricin into the victim's bloodstream.

Suddenly Markov's death read like a piece of spy theatre. An unknown assassin striking in the midst of a crowd, the murder weapon an ordinary-looking umbrella specially modified for just such a purpose, and the highly toxic ammunition almost too small to see – and, even if found, impossible to disable.

In one sense the mystery was solved before Markov had even died: broadcasting on the BBC World Service, America's Radio Free Europe and Deutsche Welle in Germany, Markov was so often critical of the Bulgarian regime that many of his fellow commuters simply assumed the Bulgarian government had decided to rid itself of him, possibly with the connivance of the KGB. But the identity of the actual killer took many years to come to light, and did so only after the fall of the Berlin Wall and its attendant upheavals. Even then the story that emerged was as tangled as any espionage thriller, with plenty of scope for a sequel.

In 1992 a former Bulgarian secret police chief received a 10-month sentence for deliberately destroying files on the Markov case. His boss, Deputy Interior Minister General Stoyan Savov, was also due to stand trial on related charges but committed suicide after a search of Bulgaria's secret service HQ uncovered a stash of similarly customised umbrellas. It was widely reported at the time that these had indeed been devised by the KGB, which had also supplied the ricin-filled pellets, although with the destruction of so much paperwork the proof of this may never be found.

Further research did indicate, however, that the Markov job had been subcontracted to a Danish hitman of Italian extraction, codenamed 'Piccadilly'. Here was a mysterious figure who had spent much of the 1970s travelling round Europe in a caravan under the guise of an art dealer. He is known to have been used for specific jobs by the Bulgarian authorities, and in 2005 was named by the *Sunday Times* as Markov's killer. The paper also described an almost identical attack on a second Bulgarian broadcaster, Vladimir Kostov, this one on the Paris Metro. Kostov had survived thanks to a thick woollen garment that prevented the toxin from properly penetrating his skin.

'Piccadilly' is known to have made three trips to London in 1977 and 1978, to have been the only pro-Bulgarian agent active in the city at that time, and to have flown out the very day after Markov was hit. He has not been seen publicly since 1993, when his house in Denmark was put on the market, and his current whereabouts remain unknown.

WAS 'GOD'S BANKER' ASSASSINATED? (1982)

BLACKFRIARS BRIDGE, EC4

WHEN THE CHAIRMAN OF ITALY'S BANCO AMBROSIANO was found hanging from Blackfriars Bridge soon after the bank's collapse, the case bore all the hallmarks of suicide. But it was nevertheless widely assumed that Roberto Calvi – immortalised in Fleet Street as 'God's Banker' thanks to his links with the Catholic Church – had been assassinated, although it took a full decade before an official enquiry reached a similar judgement, and 23 years before anyone stood trial on such a charge.

Calvi reportedly had drugs in his system, and pockets weighted down with bricks, but as a suicide it raised a number of questions. It all appeared somewhat too elaborate (why did he not just jump into the river?) and strangely public for someone who presumably could just have taken an overdose at his comfortable home in Hampstead. Interest in the case blossomed when it emerged that Calvi was a member of *Propaganda Due*, or P2, a socially prestigious and highly secretive Masonic organisation favoured by establishment figures such as politicians, newspaper editors, military officers and civil servants.

Links were soon made between this so-called 'black' lodge – whose members, interestingly, called themselves the *frati neri*, 'black friars' – and a number of other financial and corruption scandals. Official Italian masonry was quick to distance itself, pointing out that P2's charter had been withdrawn in 1976. The conspiracy theorists had long since stopped

listening, however. For them Calvi's death over water was deeply significant, symbolic of an ancient punishment designed to warn other members of the brotherhood from transgressing. For evidence of this they cited an ancient text, the first of the Masons' three blood oaths: 'O that my throat had been cut across, my tongue torn out, and my body buried in the rough sands of the sea, at low water mark, where the tide ebbs and flows twice in twenty-four hours . . .'

Calvi had been found on 19 June, nine days after fleeing Milan via Venice, a passer-by spotting his body hanging from the scaffolding under the bridge. Already implicated in what the BBC characterised as a 'complex web of international fraud and intrigue', and with a $400 million hole in the bank's accounts, he was carrying more than $14,000 in three different currencies. A verdict of suicide was reached at the inquest held the following month.

It is true that he had attempted suicide the previous year, while in prison in relation to the illegal export of several billion lire. But the official judgement following his actual death was soon overturned, replaced at first by an open verdict and then, in 2002, by a conclusion that he had been murdered.

This was reached after forensic experts appointed by the Italian courts were able to demonstrate that Calvi's neck showed none of the injuries usually associated with death by hanging, and that his hands had not come into contact with the bricks in his pockets. They also insisted that there was no evidence on Calvi's shoes or clothing to suggest that he had climbed the scaffolding, indicating that he had been killed elsewhere.

Another two years passed before the BBC reported that four people had been charged in connection with the killing and that they would stand trial in Italy. With the case expected to expose Mafia or other underworld connections to various financial scandals, the BBC confirmed that prosecutors would be attempting to prove that Calvi had been killed in order to prevent him revealing explosive secrets about Italy's political and religious establishment. At the same time it was suggested that mob bosses might have been concerned that Calvi, knowing where their money was hidden, would reveal this in the hope of reducing his sentence.

The trial duly opened in Rome in October 2005 – by which time a fifth defendant had joined the others in the dock – but in June 2007, after the jury had retired to consider its verdict, all five were acquitted. Since then no-one else has stood trial for Calvi's murder.

AN ANCIENT PUNISHMENT DESIGNED TO WARN OTHER MEMBERS OF THE BROTHERHOOD

After so many years cooperating with the Italian authorities, the City of London Police expressed their disappointment at the judgement, 'for Roberto Calvi's family in particular, that those responsible for his murder have still not faced justice'. But their concern must also have been that, once again, the tentacles of a foreign criminal power had reached deep into the capital, and managed to escape after carrying out a brutal extra-judicial killing on the streets of London.

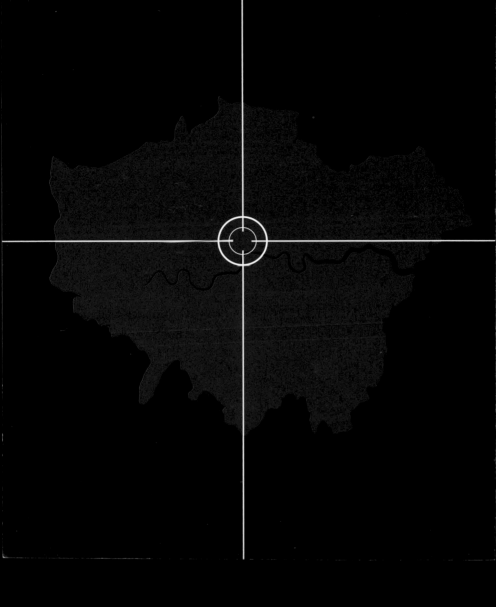

BLOOMSBURY TO COVENT GARDEN 4

MURDERS OF LONDON

PROFESSIONAL JEALOUSY HAS
TRAGIC CONSEQUENCES
(1897)

AMONG THE MANY UNEXPLAINED PRESENCES that have been reported on the London Underground – at least a dozen stations, including Aldgate, Bank and Vauxhall are said to be haunted – is a ghostly character that has been seen stalking the tunnels and platforms at Covent Garden. An imposing figure in a frock coat, tall hat, glasses and gloves, the apparition was first recorded in 1928 and then again in the 1950s, when it was suggested it could be the ghost of a Victorian actor who appeared on stage under the name William Terriss.

Terriss was born William Charles Lewin in 1847. After leaving Jesus College, Oxford, without graduating, he tried his hand at several different careers around the world, including sheep farming Down Under, tea planting in the Indian subcontinent, prospecting for precious metals in the Americas, and even medicine. Eventually he decided to return home and take to the stage.

His energy, adventurous personality and naturally swashbuckling demeanour seemed to stand him in good stead professionally, and a run of popular and remunerative appearances followed in shows based on such box-office favourites as *Ivanhoe* and *Robin Hood*. Terriss also took on Shakespeare, playing Cassio in *Othello* and eventually the lead in *Romeo and Juliet*. In short, Terriss proved to be a great success in a risky

ADELPHI

CITY OF WESTMINSTER
WILLIAM TERRISS
1847 - 1897
HERO OF THE ADELPHI
MELODRAMAS

MET HIS UNTIMELY END
OUTSIDE THIS THEATRE
16 DEC 1897

THE ADELPHI THEATRE CO. LTD

business. After touring the US in a number of productions in 1885 with his lover Jessie Millward, he returned to London, where he was rarely without work.

He subsequently married the actress Amy Fellowes, producing a son, Tom (who followed his parents into the business, becoming an actor, writer and later film director), and a daughter, actress Ellaline Terriss, who married the theatre proprietor Seymour Hicks. The latter owned two theatres in the West End, at one of which – the Adelphi – his father-in-law was booked in December 1897 to appear in William Gillette's melodrama

Secret Service. Terriss arrived here for work as usual on the evening of the 16th, but on stepping up to what is now the stage door on Maiden Lane was violently accosted by Richard Prince, a young bit-part actor, who without warning stabbed the 50-year-old to death.

Coming out of the blue as it did, the murder caused a sensation. Terriss was dead within minutes but his assailant was seized and held by passers-by until the police arrived. Prince was quick to confess, telling officers, 'He has had due warning, and if he is dead, he knew what to expect from me.'

It transpired that Prince, 20 years his victim's junior, was well known to Terriss, who had made repeated attempts to further his career. On a number of occasions he had managed to get the younger man small parts in shows in which he himself took the leading role, but Prince's drinking and occasionally erratic behaviour meant that this was becoming harder to do. With Prince growing increasingly resentful and jealous of Terriss things reached a head in early December when his former mentor was forced to arrange for him to be dismissed. On the 13th Prince was asked in no uncertain terms to leave the Vaudeville Theatre, and shortly afterwards the two men were heard arguing in a dressing room at the Adelphi. Possibly the row was over money, as Terriss had previously negotiated for Prince to receive help from the Actors' Benevolent Fund in nearby Adam Street. For some reason the money was not forthcoming that day and, concluding that Terriss was to blame for this latest slight, Prince had hastened across the Strand to the Adelphi.

In so far as it was a premeditated attack, Prince might have been expected to hang, but following his arrest it was quickly determined that – besides being jealous of Terriss and convinced that he, Prince, deserved much better roles than he was being offered – Richard Prince was in fact insane. With no real case to answer he was quietly committed to the Criminal Lunatic Asylum at Broadmoor, the apparent leniency of his punishment infuriating theatre-goers and actors alike, who were not to know that he would stay locked up there until his death 40 years later aged 71.

The Actors' Benevolent Fund still survives, and today its own website refers to the case, suggesting that Prince 'spent the rest of his days producing plays with himself as the leading character and the other inmates in supporting roles'. Terriss, meanwhile, continues to captivate audiences of a different kind, if not at Covent Garden station then at the Adelphi, where his ghost is also said to tread the boards from time to time. A plaque at the rear of the theatre records his murder.

'BLODIE BELGIAM'
– A TRULY BOTCHED COVER UP
(1917)

- **101 CHARLOTTE STREET, W1**
- **50 MUNSTER SQUARE, NW1**

ON 2 NOVEMBER 1917 a roadsweeper working his early-morning beat in Regent Square, St Pancras, came upon a package that had been thrown over the railings into the private central garden. Unwrapping an outer layer of what looked like sacking he discovered a female trunk and arms. The police were called and shortly afterwards found the victim's legs in another parcel elsewhere in the square.

There was no sign of the head or hands, but while the victim's identity was yet to be established there were plenty of clues. Lettering on the hessian sack read 'Argentina La Plata Cold Storage' – a reference to a meat-packing plant – with one parcel also containing a bedsheet with a clearly identifiable laundry mark, scraps of muslin, some ladies' underwear and a piece of paper bearing the legend 'blodie Belgiam'.

The laundry mark led the police straight to the home of a 32-year-old Frenchwoman named Emilienne Gerard, who had not been seen for three days. In her rooms at 50 Munster Square they found a few small bloodstains, an IOU for £50 signed 'Louis Voisin', and a picture of a stocky, powerfully built man who was assumed to be M. Voisin.

CHARLOTTE STREET

MUNSTER SQUARE

Quickly traced to his basement flat in Charlotte Street, Voisin turned out to be another French ex-pat who was working as a butcher. This last observation was particularly interesting as an examination of the remains in Regent Square suggested the dismembering was the work of an expert – and muslin was at this time commonly used by butchers to wrap joints of meat. Voisin soon found himself at Bow Street helping the police with their enquiries, as did his companion Berthe Roche.

The evidence against Voisin was from the start compelling. He knew and had visited Mme Gerard on numerous occasions, had a key to Munster Square and was paying her rent. Asked in the interview to write out 'bloody Belgium', he made the same spelling mistakes five times in succession. He also had another key, to the coal cellar beneath the pavement outside 101 Charlotte Street, in which police found a barrel containing Mme Gerard's hands and head. Finally a more detailed search of his own property uncovered several more bloodstains and a single earring.

A Home Office pathologist's report, prepared by the eminent Sir Bernard Spilsbury, revealed that Mme Gerard had been struck in the head and face a minimum of eight times, and then been strangled while a towel was held over her mouth to stifle her cries. It is assumed the earring had been lost during this struggle, which had clearly taken place at Charlotte Street rather than at Munster Square.

It did not take long for the truth to emerge, which was that the victim had ducked into her friend Voisin's basement to shelter from an air raid on the last night of October. She found him in the company of Roche and the two women quickly came to blows, during which altercation Mme Gerard was hit repeatedly with a poker. It was Sir Bernard's opinion that this improvised weapon must have been wielded by Roche rather than Voisin, who, being stronger, would almost certainly have killed her outright. Voisin, however, had probably been responsible for silencing the victim with the towel, and possibly for strangling her. Certainly he was responsible for the skilled dissection, for the disposal of the body – which had briefly been stored at Munster Square, hence the traces of blood there – and for the chillingly inept attempt at disguising the killing as a racist attack at a time of war.

With such a strong connection between perpetrator and victim, a clear motive, forensic evidence carelessly left all over the place and body parts liberally scattered around central London, it is hard to believe that Roche and Voisin could ever have imagined they might get away with their crime. That said, in a sense the former did. Charged only as an accessory after the fact, Berthe Roche received a sentence of only seven years, of which she served just one-and-a-half before going insane and dying of natural causes. Voisin, however, was to feel the full weight of the law: on 2 March the following year he dropped through the hatch at Pentonville and was pronounced dead aged 43.

Unfortunately all three addresses have now disappeared, the whole of Munster and most of Regent Square undergoing complete redevelopment after being largely destroyed in the Blitz, while the butcher's address in Charlotte Street is now just a scruffy, litter-strewn service entrance to a residential block attached to University College, London.

THE DEATH OF AN
EGYPTIAN PRINCELING
(1923)

THE MEDIA LOVE A GOOD MURDER, and rarely more so than when an aristocrat is involved. In 2004, for instance, the disappearance of the 10th Earl of Shaftesbury had all the makings of a perfect (if tragic) tabloid whodunnit, particularly when a body was discovered hidden in the French Alps and all the evidence pointed to his own wife, an exotically-named former nightclub hostess.

In 1923 a similarly juicy story emerged much closer to home, and, although the protagonists gave it a hint of mysterious Eastern glamour, the action was set against the backdrop of London's Savoy Hotel. It was outside a suite in this celebrated hotel that Ali Kamel Fahmi Bey was found shot to death.

The fabulously rich Egyptian princeling had married a Frenchwoman, Marguerite, who, after confessing to having shot the prince, found herself at Bow Street Magistrates Court. Once there Madame Fahmi's glittering diamonds and emeralds attracted just as much comment as the details of her late husband's demise in the early hours of 10 July.

The case is most noteworthy, however, for Madame Fahmi's surprise acquittal. She had never troubled to deny that she had a gun in the hotel, nor that she had fired it at her husband. She nevertheless escaped a conviction even for manslaughter after what has been described as

a truly bravura performance by her barrister, Sir Edward Marshall Hall, who had shrewdly gauged that his client's best chance lay in an open appeal to the jury's solidly racist instincts.

The couple had married just eight months earlier, Marguerite something of a gold-digger who must have considered the handsome 22-year-old Egyptian quite a catch. Strictly speaking, Fahmi was a nobleman rather than a prince, but when travelling abroad neither of them troubled to put anyone right. Theirs was evidently something of a fiery relationship, and witnesses spoke of seeing Ali's scratched face and Marguerite's ill-concealed bruises. Shortly after checking into the Savoy on this occasion, Madame had summoned the hotel doctor and showed him some minor injuries, which she blamed on her husband's preference for what she described as 'unnatural intercourse'. Perhaps already thinking of divorce, she had requested of him some kind of certificate relating to her condition.

On 9 July the couple went to the theatre – as it happens, to see *The Merry Widow* – and were afterwards observed arguing loudly in the hotel dining room. With each threatening the other with a beating from an empty wine bottle, they were eventually pacified by the *maître d'*, after which Madame Fahmi briefly took in the house band in the ballroom and then went up to bed alone.

At 2am three shots were heard, the night porter later relating that he had found Ali bleeding heavily from a head wound and his wife, having dropped a black handgun, saying over and over, '*Qu'est-ce que j'ai fait, mon cher?*' ('What have I done, my dear?').

In court the following September, Sir Edward lost no opportunity in portraying the victim as a violent and immoral alien, a sinister foreigner with 'abnormal tendencies' who as likely as not was engaged in a gross and illegal relationship with his male secretary. He was, said Sir Edward, an Oriental given to a life of debauchery and 'obsessed with his sexual prowess', and his crime was to regard his wife as merely another possession to be used and abused at will. Thereafter the proceedings were never anything but unbalanced in her favour, the judge on the one hand allowing a description of the potentate's household as a conspiracy of 'numerous ugly, black, half-civilised manservants', and on the other refusing permission for the prosecution even to cross-examine Madame Fahmi.

'QU'EST-CE QUE J'AI FAIT, MON CHER?'

In the end it was left to Sir Edward to deal the final blow, observing that, while 'we in this country put our women on a pedestal, in Egypt they have not the same views.' Addressing the all-white jury he implored them 'to open the gate and let this white woman go back into the light of God's great Western sun'. To the undisguised fury of the Egyptian Ambassador in London the jury agreed, allowing Madame Fahmi to leave the court a free woman.

Press opinion across the Middle East was one of outrage, and the venerable *Al-Ahram* fumed at descriptions of Egypt's 'backwardness' and 'barbarity'. Closer to home, Madame Fahmi's good fortune took a knock when details emerged about her time as a prostitute and a 15-year-old unmarried mother. Such as it was her reputation never recovered. Unable to inherit her husband's reputed £2 million fortune she found herself a laughing stock when she returned home to Paris. In January 1971, she died at the age of 81, more or less a recluse.

THE CHARING CROSS TRUNK MURDER (1927)

- **CHARING CROSS STATION, STRAND, WC2**
- **86 ROCHESTER ROW, SW1**

THE NAME OF THE MURDERER may be all but forgotten, and the precise details of his crime a little hazy, but the phrase 'Charing Cross Trunk Murder' still presses all the right buttons to rank alongside Rillington Place (p.240) or the Ratcliffe Highway (p.10).

On 6 May 1927, after leaving a substantial black trunk and very specific instructions as to its handling, a man walked out of the left-luggage office at Charing Cross station, climbed into a cab and disappeared along the Strand. The staff thought no more about it until a few days later, when a dreadful smell was traced to the trunk and the police were called.

With a sense of foreboding, the trunk was opened on 10 May, revealing a dismembered corpse with each of the limbs individually wrapped in brown paper. An examination of the remains, once again by Sir Bernard Spilsbury (p.86), determined that the body was that of a woman: she was stocky, about 35 years old, and had bruising to the stomach, back and forehead that had been inflicted while she was unconscious. The address on the trunk drew a blank, but not for the first time a laundry mark provided a useful clue by suggesting the corpse belonged to a 'Mrs Roles'.

Investigations continued, and after an appeal was published in the London dailies a shopkeeper in Brixton supplied police with a description

ROCHESTER ROW

CHARING CROSS STATION

of a mustachioed man in his mid-30s who had bought just such a trunk. At the same time a cab driver came forward saying he had helped load a trunk into his cab for transfer to Charing Cross. His description of his fare sounded remarkably similar to that provided by the shopkeeper.

The cabbie's pick-up had been at 86 Rochester Row near Victoria, where police found the hastily vacated but scrupulously clean office – suspiciously clean, even – of 35-year-old estate agent John Robinson. He had not been seen by his fellow tenants since the 6th but was soon tracked down to an address in De Laune Street, Kennington, and was taken to Scotland Yard for questioning.

'I WANT TO TELL YOU ALL ABOUT IT. I DONE IT AND CUT HER UP'

Initially Robinson denied all knowledge of the crime, and neither the shopkeeper nor the cab driver were able to pick him out in an identity parade – even though, with his neat turnout and military bearing, his appearance was very much akin to their recollections. Robinson was therefore released and only later changed his story when another, more careful search of the third-floor premises turned up a matchstick in the bin on which was a tiny trace of blood.

Officers now thought that, having killed and dismembered his victim, the murderer had painstakingly cleaned the office to get rid of the evidence, but then carelessly discarded the match after sitting back to enjoy a well-earned cigarette. Robinson was rearrested, and this time decided he may as well spill the beans. 'I want to tell you all about it,' he told the detective who interviewed him. 'I done it and cut her up.'

'Mrs Roles' turned out to be Minnie Bonati, the former wife of an Italian waiter, who was in the habit of supplementing her work as a domestic servant with a little part-time prostitution. Robinson said she had approached him outside Victoria Station and the two had returned to his rented office in Rochester Row. A quarrel took place, presumably about money, during which she had been suffocated by his attempts to quieten her.

It is tempting to suppose that, had he crossed the road to Rochester Road police station at this point and explained what had happened, Robinson might have escaped with a charge of manslaughter. This is on the assumption that the death actually appeared to have been accidental. Instead he panicked and ran out into the street to buy a large kitchen knife, which he then used to dismember the corpse. Bonati's constituent parts were then packed into a cheap 12-shilling trunk, which he deposited at Charing Cross station.

Robinson's late confession, and the very considered efforts he went to to conceal his crime, left him little room for manoeuvre at his trial on 11 July at the Old Bailey. Witnesses testified that the victim was a violent alcoholic, but it took the jury less than an hour to find John Robinson guilty of killing her. He was hanged at Pentonville on 12 August. The office at no.86 disappeared long ago, but the row of shops opposite the brown-brick office block that now occupies the site gives a good impression of how it would have looked in the 1920s.

GANG VIOLENCE
CLAIMS AN INNOCENT VICTIM (1947)

- **73-75 CHARLOTTE STREET, W1**
- **CHARLOTTE STREET/TOTTENHAM STREET JUNCTION, W1**

POPULARLY SUPPOSED TO HAVE BEEN WITNESSED by hangman Albert Pierrepoint as he enjoyed a drink at the Fitzroy Tavern, the cold-blooded murder of motorcycle mechanic and father of six Alec de Antiquis in broad daylight on a West End street created a wave of fear across the capital. At the time, speculation was rife that gun crime and gang violence were getting out of control – which sounds perfectly indisputable until we recall that this incident took place in 1947 rather than the present day.

Shortly after 2.30 p.m. on 29 April, the 31-year-old de Antiquis had been gunned down as he attempted to waylay three armed robbers making their escape from Jay's Jewellers on Charlotte Street, Fitzrovia. When their black Vauxhall's escape route was blocked by traffic, the gang managed successfully to disappear into the crowds, sparking one of the largest manhunts London had yet seen.

Violent crime in the capital was experiencing something of a peak in the immediate post-war period, in part (it has been argued) because a flood of handguns had come onto the market at the close of hostilities. Droves of former servicemen, now unemployed, had turned to crime after being demobbed, while a whole generation of poorly educated delinquents had grown up with their fathers away fighting. A recent weapons amnesty had succeeded in taking more than 18,000 illegally held guns out of

CHARLOTTE STREET

CHARLOTTE STREET/
TOTTENHAM STREET JUNCTION

circulation on a single day, but, with possession of a weapon sometimes attracting fines of only a couple of pounds or less, armed attacks in central London were still on the rise. Against this background the death of the Anglo-Italian de Antiquis must have been a gift to the press, his story one of an innocent bystander attempting to prevent a crime, a young husband and father standing up for justice against a criminal element that seemed to be getting the upper hand.

In just such a vein one newspaper described how, his red motorcycle abandoned at the junction with Tottenham Street, 'a dead man lies on a London pavement . . . a sight we associate with Chicago but not with the capital of Britain'. Others editorialised about the unwelcome influence of the latest wave of mobster films from Hollywood, and the lenient punishments being handed out by the courts to anyone who sought to emulate this new class of American antihero.

Scotland Yard responded by putting one of its best men, Chief Inspector Robert Fabian, on the case. He quickly tracked down his three suspects using a combination of painstaking forensic examination and careful referencing and cross-referencing of the huge mass of information he and his men had been able to gather. Before long a gun was recovered from the muddy shore of the Thames, and, while witness statements often proved contradictory, a taxi driver recalled seeing two men running into Brook House, a building on Tottenham Court Road, shortly after the attack. At Brook House police found a discarded raincoat belonging to Charles Henry Jenkins, a 23-year-old with definite 'form'.

The arrest of two of his associates quickly followed, both of them – Christopher James Geraghty (aged 21) and Terence Peter Rolt (17) – fingering the older man at the first chance they got. All three found themselves in the dock on 21 July charged with murder, and within a week all three had been found guilty. Being of age, Jenkins and Geraghty were sentenced to death, and were hanged side by side at Pentonville on 19 September 1947. The underage Rolt escaped a similar fate, however, and was instead detained at His Majesty's pleasure before being released on licence after serving nine and a half years.

The jewellers on Charlotte Street is long gone, the site now home to a contraception clinic, and more than 60 years later the murder, its perpetrators and victim have been more or less forgotten. But their story cast a long shadow, providing the inspiration for an Ealing Studios production called *The Blue Lamp*, which opened in 1950. In it a gunman (played by Dirk Bogarde) fleeing the scene of a crime shoots dead a policeman who attempts to arrest him. The film set the template for the fictional 'British bobby', and its spin-offs included two new television dramas: *Fabian of the Yard*, and the even more successful *Dixon of Dock Green*. The latter saw the murdered policeman restored to health and able to apprehend petty criminals well into the mid-1970s.

'A DEAD MAN LIES ON A LONDON PAVEMENT'

THE FIRST
IDENTIKIT MURDERER
(1961)

23 CECIL COURT, WC2

BRIEFLY HOME TO THE YOUNG MOZART and his family in 1764 and later the location of the first Foyles bookshop before it moved to Charing Cross Road, Cecil Court has long been a Mecca for bibliophiles as well as a useful shortcut for non-readers making their way west from St Martin's Lane.

On 3 March 1961 Cecil Court hit the headlines when an assistant at Louis Meier's antique shop was discovered brutally murdered at the back of the premises. Fifty-nine-year-old Elsie May Batten had multiple stab wounds, from two of which protruded the ivory handles of pair of antique daggers. Her employer had not been present at the time of the attack, but it was he who called the police on discovering the body. Later that day the victim was identified by her husband, Mark Batten, a distinguished sculptor whose statue *Diogenist* can still be seen in Golders Hill Park, NW11.

Questioned by detectives, the shop owner recalled a visit the previous day by a young man of mixed race who had expressed an interest in a curved dress sword and in two antique daggers. He had left without buying anything but the sword was now missing, and the antique daggers were now important pieces of evidence.

From Mr Meier's recollections, Bow Street's Detective Sergeant Raymond Dagg was able to produce a hand-drawn 'identikit' likeness of the mysterious visitor using a system newly arrived from North America.

Dagg also interviewed neighbouring shopkeepers, one of whom said he had been approached by a young man, possibly Indian, who had attempted to sell him a sword for £15. He too provided a description from which the police officer drafted a second identikit image. The similarity between the two drawings was striking, and posters showing the two images side by side were circulated to police stations and the press. Just five days after the murder a policeman on duty in Old Compton Street had a lucky break when he collared a man who closely matched the descriptions given by Meier and his Cecil Court neighbour. Twenty-one-year-old Edwin Bush, who was taken into custody with his girlfriend, became the first murderer in Britain to be apprehended using an identikit image.

SPEAKING PERSONALLY
THE WORLD IS BETTER
OFF WITHOUT ME

Although Bush himself agreed that the identikit pictures bore a certain likeness, he denied having any connection with Cecil Court or the late Mrs Batten, but he was subsequently unable to substantiate the alibi he claimed to have for the day in question. Louis Meier failed to pick him out of an identity parade but Paul Roberts confirmed that Bush was the young man who had offered to sell him the sword for £15.

At this point Bush agreed to cooperate, and thereafter provided a full sword but had lost his nerve, picked up a stone vase and hit Mrs Batten. 'I don't know what came over me,' he said. 'Speaking personally the world is better off without me.'

Ahead of his trial, background checks revealed an all-too-familiar picture. The defendants' childhood living conditions had been sufficiently poor to warrant an investigation by the NSPCC, and he had subsequently spent a period in a children's home and several spells in borstal for housebreaking and theft.

This latest crime was particularly brutal and wholly unprovoked, however, and during the trial at the Old Bailey in May 1961 the verdict must have seemed almost a formality. So too the sentence, since the murder of Mrs Batten had been committed in the 'course or furtherance of theft', a capital offence specifically referenced in the 1957 Homicide Act. Indeed, proceedings took less than two days to complete, and Bush was hanged at Pentonville on 6 July.

The shop in Cecil Court still exists, as a bookseller's, and having played such an historic and pioneering role in murder detection the two identikit images were lodged in the National Archives, under the Catalogue reference CRIM 1/3661.

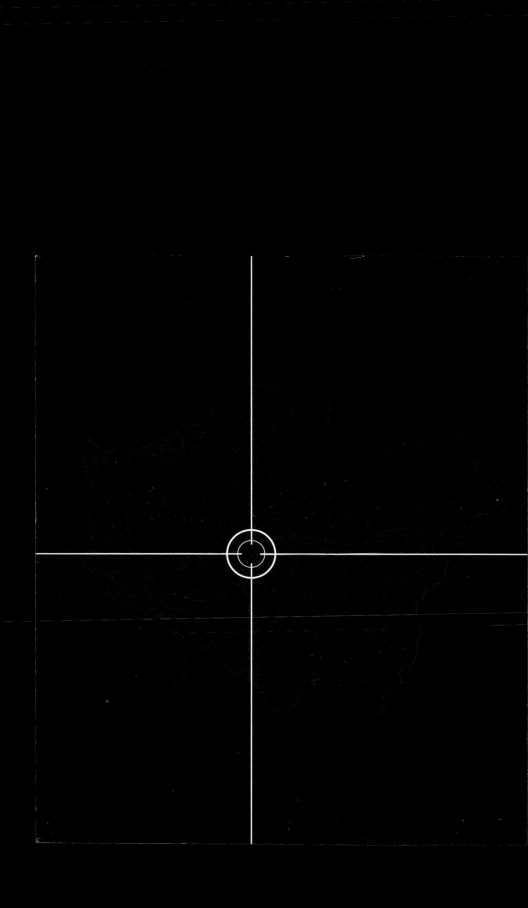

KENSINGTON
& CHELSEA 5

MURDERS OF LONDON

A HANDYMAN'S
ILL-THOUGHT-OUT PLANS
(1870)

- **24 WELLINGTON SQUARE, SW3**
- **15 PAULTONS SQUARE, SW3**

A MATCHING PAIR OF VIOLENT, unprovoked and readily solved crimes, the so-called Chelsea Murders were committed by a handyman with so obvious a connection to the victims that one struggles to imagine even how he could have expected to get away with it.

The handyman was 31-year-old Scotsman Walter Miller, and on 9 May 1870 he was working for 84-year-old Elias Huelin, an occasional assistant chaplain at Brompton Cemetery. In particular Miller had been charged with finishing some plastering at a property in Wellington Square. When Reverend Huelin called at the house that morning to see how work was progressing, however, he was hit over the head with a spade and crammed into a cupboard, having being searched and relieved of any valuables.

Huelin, an ex-pat French protestant, had owned this house as well as another slightly smaller one in Paultons Square, a few minutes' walk away. Having concealed the body in this hasty fashion, Miller set off down the King's Road, apparently determined to surprise the clergyman's housekeeper and do away with her, too. At the second address he found said housekeeper, Mrs Ann Boss, and strangled her with a length of rope before hiding her away in a large wooden box.

PAULTONS SQUARE

WELLINGTON SQUARE

In so far as he had a plan, Miller had apparently hoped to rob the houses of anything he could turn into cash, and then, by passing himself off as Huelin's nephew – newly arrived from Jersey and sporting an obviously dyed beard – somehow secure legal entitlement to the two properties and to any others Huelin had in the vicinity. Before he could put this final stage into operation, however, Miller felt he had earned a drink and to this end he spent much of the following day taking cabs from one tavern to the next. By buying drinks for anyone who wanted one and affecting a very poor and ever-declining imitation of what he assumed to be a French accent, he had soon managed quite effectively to draw attention to himself at a time when a smarter man might have gone to ground.

Although Miller did not know it yet, there were already concerns about the old clergyman: one witness in the King's Road, having seen his old friend step off an omnibus and go into Wellington Square, was wondering why he had not seen him emerge. At the same time, Miller had asked a workman to go round to the house in order to lift a drain, even though the owner was nowhere to be seen when the man got there.

Miller's next mistake was to ask a local greengrocer, Henry Piper, if he would bring his cart to the Paultons Square house to help remove some of the effects. When Piper arrived and asked how much he was to be paid for doing this, Miller answered, somewhat strangely, 'Me pay you anything you charge. You make your charge and I will pay.' Among the things to be moved was the large wooden box containing Mrs Boss, which had been firmly strapped shut. But on lifting it Piper felt a damp sensation on his hands and realised the box was covered with fresh blood, which had also pooled on the floor below.

When he questioned Miller about this, the latter's accent slipped. Piper was able to manoeuvre him up the basement stairs and out into the square, but by now it was raining hard and Miller was able to break free. As he made a run for it, Piper alerted a constable who was sheltering under a nearby lamp and the Scotsman was soon on his way to the police station.

Meanwhile a sergeant returned to the house with Piper and used a fire poker to break open the chest, in which he found the remains of Mrs Boss with a length of clothes line still knotted around her neck. A thorough search of the house uncovered the body of Rev. Huelin, which had been taken from the cupboard and stuffed into the newly excavated drain.

After his formal arrest, Miller took poison he had apparently procured from a local chemist the afternoon of the second murder, presumably anticipating that such an ill-conceived plan might fail. But after a short stay in St George's Hospital – now remodelled as the Lanesborough Hotel – the presumed double murderer was considered fit enough to plead. His trial at the Old Bailey commenced on 11 July.

Miller made a brief attempt to blame the killings on the nephew he had invented and then impersonated, but this failed and he was sentenced to death. The same judge ordered a payment of £50 to be made to Henry Piper for his quick thinking and courage.

'YOU MAKE YOUR CHARGE AND I WILL PAY'

A RUSSIAN
DOUBLE-AGENT
MEETS HIS END (1933)

31 PEMBROKE GARDENS, W8

THE VICTIM OF THE FIRST OF MANY espionage-related murders in the
Royal Borough, Ernest Holloway Oldham appeared to most people to be
an unimportant middle-ranking civil servant. In reality, he was secretly
in the employ of the OGPU – Stalin's secret police, a forerunner of the
KGB – and is now known to have spied against Britain in the 1920s and
early 1930s.

Oldham was a mercenary volunteer to the communist cause rather
than an ideological recruit from the colleges of Cambridge University.
Officially he worked as a cipher clerk at the Foreign Office, but he had
been driven to seek more lucrative employment after running into
money problems that were exacerbated by his prolific alcohol and
drug habit. Colleagues, intrigued as to how he was able to maintain an
attractive detached house in a smart part of town as well as a uniformed
chauffeur, assumed he must have a private income, but the truth was
somewhat darker.

On a trip to Paris in late 1927 or early 1928, Oldham had presented
himself at the Russian Embassy, calling himself 'Mr Scott' and offering his
services. Unsurprisingly, perhaps, the offer was rejected, the Soviets quite
sure that such a straightforward approach could be nothing but a clumsy

and amateurish effort at infiltration by the British security services. Undeterred, Oldham made a second visit, this time receiving a more cordial welcome, having in the meantime been able to demonstrate the value of the information that passed through his hands back in London. No immediate agreement was reached, but a few months later an agent known as 'Galleni' was dispatched to London with instructions to locate and recruit the mysterious Mr Scott.

Incredibly, Galleni engaged the Metropolitan Police to help him track his man down, providing them with the date of an alleged minor car accident in Paris with an unnamed British civil servant. The police helpfully supplied the home addresses of several Foreign Office officials who were known to have been in Paris at the time, thanks to which Galleni soon struck gold in Pembroke Gardens.

COMPLETELY IN THE HANDS OF THE OGPU

Galleni reportedly handed Oldham £2,000 in cash and a relationship was quickly established – only for it to hit the buffers soon afterwards as Oldham's drinking got more and more out of hand. In 1932 he lost his Foreign Office job after being caught drunk once too often, a catastrophic development that left him – in the words of an official MI5 file later produced on the case – 'completely in the hands of the OGPU'. The same file goes on to note how, in desperate financial straits, Oldham 'continued to obtain Foreign Office material by making use of his previous position there'. It seems Whitehall security was so slack that a former employee who had been dismissed for drunkenness was somehow still permitted to visit his old office, converse with old colleagues and even store personal items in the 'confidential presses', or office safe.

Oldham's controller at the OGPU must have been amazed when he heard this, and presumably would have kept paying him while useful snippets of intelligence continued to flow from London to Paris via Galleni. But with Oldham's addiction to drugs and alcohol dramatically reducing his usefulness to the Soviets and repeatedly trying Galleni's patience, his days were sadly numbered. At one point Galleni even threatened to expose his own agent to MI5 unless he shaped up and got a grip. It is possible that the hapless Oldham was by this stage unable to help himself. The MI5 files suggest he was having some kind of breakdown, describing how on one occasion – while meeting his Soviet handler in the dark obscurity of a cinema – he caused a scene because Galleni neglected to get to his feet when 'God Save the King' was played.

Not long after this, Oldham was suspected of making copies of the cipher room keys when a set was returned by him to Whitehall with traces of wax or soap clearly visible. It seems incredible that he would have had an opportunity to do this, but at last his erstwhile employers put him under MI5 surveillance. A few days later he was found dead in the flat at Pembroke Gardens, dressed in nightclothes with his head in the oven.

Officially the death was described as suicide, a case of man who had no desire to face his creditors, or who perhaps took the obvious way out after realising that MI5 was onto him. But just as likely, the MI5 file admits, is that, having exhausted his usefulness, Oldham was bumped off by Stalin's agents sensibly covering their tracks.

JOHN HAIGH -
THE ACID BATH MURDERER
(1949)

● **79 GLOUCESTER ROAD, SW7**
● **THE GOAT, 3 KENSINGTON HIGH STREET, W8**

THE GRISLY REPUTATION OF THE DAPPER serial killer John Haigh depends less on his actual crimes than on the means by which he chose to conceal them. Popularly branded the Kensington Vampire after admitting to drinking the blood of his victims, Haigh is better known as the Acid Bath Murderer.

It is quite likely that that vampire claim was nothing more than a desperate bid by Haigh to feign insanity and escape the noose. Otherwise he made little attempt to help himself after his arrest, even going so far as to suggest that he had committed nine murders rather than the one for which he first came under suspicion. The precise extent of his crimes will probably never be known, since he rid himself of the bodies by dissolving them in drums of concentrated prussic acid and pouring the residue down a drain.

Also known as hydrogen cyanide, prussic acid is highly toxic and extremely corrosive, something Haigh demonstrated to his own satisfaction by dissolving several mice in it after conceiving of his plan while in prison on a charge of fraud. As a small-scale manufacturer of false fingernails, the former Wakefield Cathedral chorister had access to the necessary quantities of acid, which he kept in a basement workshop on Gloucester

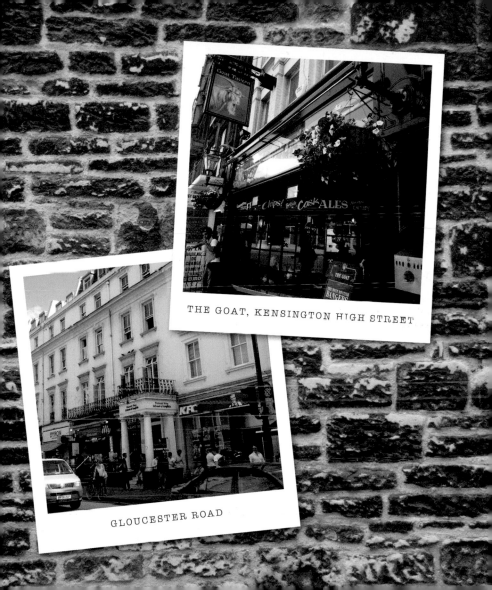

THE GOAT, KENSINGTON HIGH STREET

GLOUCESTER ROAD

Road beneath what is now a language school and – with a grim sort of irony – a Kentucky Fried Chicken.

His first victim was William Donald McSwann, an acquaintance he bumped into by chance at The Goat in Kensington High Street. Inviting McSwann back to his basement on 6 September 1944, Haigh knocked him unconscious, doubtless taking some pleasure in the successful prosecution of a carefully-thought-out scheme, although his motivation was also partly mercenary. Having met McSwann's parents he knew them to be well off. He also knew they would probably try to enlist his help in locating their missing son. Sure enough, ten months later, they too found their way to the basement, where they were dispatched in a similarly brutal manner. After forging documents that appeared to give him power of attorney over the McSwann estate, Haigh moved into the nearby Onslow Court Hotel, where he set himself up as a successful businessman about town by selling around £4,000 worth of McSwann properties.

It was at the Onslow Court – now Jury's Kensington Hotel – that Haigh befriended Olivia Durand-Deacon, a wealthy widow of 69. Having managed to interest her in the technicalities of artificial nail production, Haigh invited her to a second workshop he had rented at Leopold Road, Crawley. Here he killed her, dismembered her body and set it to dissolve in a 40-gallon container of acid before returning to London with her jewellery, which, again, he sold.

Unfortunately for Haigh, the widow may have been lonely but she was not without friends, and her sudden and unexplained disappearance led another hotel resident, Constance Lane, to take her suspicions to the police. Acting on a hunch, one of the detectives did a bit of digging around, discovering in pretty short order that Haigh had convictions for fraud, selling stolen cars and looting bombed-out buildings. He was also in arrears at the hotel, suggesting money troubles.

Haigh at first refused to cooperate when he was brought in for questioning, but then surprised one of the investigating officers by asking, 'What are the chances of anyone getting out of Broadmoor?' He subsequently appeared to confess, although he seemed confident that the lack of a body ruled out a court case or conviction. But Haigh had not reckoned with the determination of Detective Inspector Shelley-Symes and the tenacity of Home Office pathologist Dr Keith Simpson. Simpson's painstaking examination of the two workshops soon uncovered more than 28 pounds of a suspiciously greasy substance – later identified as human fat – as well as three gallstones, a readily identifiable set of female dentures and 18 fragments of human bone.

'WHAT ARE THE CHANCES OF ANYONE GETTING OUT OF BROADMOOR?'

Haigh's trial lasted just two days and saw him charged with only one murder, even though he confessed to eight more, including a Dr Henderson and his wife, a woman from Hammersmith and another he said he had met at Eastbourne. His lawyers argued forcefully that he was insane, pointing to a traumatic childhood of bullying at the hands of his fanatically strict Plymouth Brethren parents. Haigh himself displayed what a medical witness described as a 'callous, cheerful, bland and almost friendly indifference', and the jury remained unpersuaded.

Come the second day, the jury took just 17 minutes to convict. On the bright, sunny morning of 10 August 1949, London's Acid Bath Murderer was hanged by the neck at Wandsworth.

THE TRAGIC AND LONELY TALE OF
CHRISTINE GRANVILLE
(1952)

A BEAUTIFUL AND ACCOMPLISHED wartime agent who provided the model for at least two Bond girls – Vespa Lynd and Tatiana Romanova – Krystyna Skarbek was the daughter of a Polish count and distantly related to the composer Chopin. She adopted the nom de guerre Christine Granville when she was recruited into Britain's Special Operations Executive in 1940, and chose to keep it when she settled in London after the war.

Granville's skills as a spy are well documented, and it has been suggested that her success in the role helped persuade the authorities that the SOE might profit by recruiting more women for espionage and sabotage work in occupied Europe. Exceptionally resourceful, she once escaped from the Gestapo after faking the symptoms of tuberculosis by biting her tongue until it bled, while in July 1944 she was parachuted into France and assisted a joint force of Italian partisans and French *maquis* in harrying the Germans in the Alps. She was also credited with saving the lives of several SOE colleagues by bribing the officer who proposed shooting them and persuading him that, as the niece of General Montgomery, she would ensure he was targeted for special retribution. She was no such thing and only later realised quite how much danger she had put herself in. 'What have I done?' she asked. 'They could have shot me as well.'

On 15 June 1952, the 44-year-old checked into her hotel in Lexham Gardens. There she was confronted by Muldowney, who questioned her about a trip she was planning to see a former lover and SOE comrade, the one-legged Polish war hero Andrzej Kowerski, and ultimately pulled out a knife. The hotel's night porter later described how he had run to Granville's aid after hearing her shout, 'Get him off me!' – but he was too late. Granville was already dead of a chest wound. Muldowney freely admitted that he had killed her and waited quietly while the police were summoned. When the officers arrived he confessed to the crime, telling them angrily, 'I built all my dreams around her, but she was playing me for a fool.'

Brought to court at the Old Bailey Muldowney stuck by this version of events and insisted that 'to kill is the final possession.' This, as well as his guilty plea, ensured that his murder trial was one of the shortest on record: a mere three minutes from start to finish.

Muldowney went to Pentonville and was hanged on 30 September 1952, with the press describing his victim as 'the modern pimpernel no man could resist'. To them and to the public Granville's story proved irresistible, even without the 007 connection, and at the time of writing newspapers in both Britain and Poland were abuzz with talk of a new movie starring Eva Green – Vesper Lynd in the remake of *Casino Royale* – as Christine Granville.

KENNETH GILBERT AND IAN GRANT,
GOOD FRIENDS TO THE END (1954)

ABAN COURT HOTEL, 25 HARRINGTON GARDENS, SW7

WHETHER IT IS BETTER TO BE HANGED ALONE or in the company of a good friend is happily one of life's imponderables, although to most the thought of two men being hanged side by side is even more chilling than the two of them being dispatched out of sight of each other. For a long time, though, double hangings were considered acceptable for partners in crime, and the practice was not outlawed until the Homicide Act of 1957, which determined that, where more than one person was to be hanged for the same offence, the prisoners would be executed simultaneously but at different prisons. As a result of this ruling, Gilbert and Grant are today remembered as the last two to receive their punishment in the old-fashioned manner.

The duo's brutally clumsy handiwork was first observed by kitchen staff at the Aban Court Hotel in Kensington, who arrived for work on the morning of 9 March 1954 to find the body of a colleague, George Smart, bound, gagged and stuffed in the servery. Despite a considerable head injury, the 55-year-old night porter had struggled to free himself, managing to release his arms but then suffocating on the gag.

Robbery appeared to be the motive rather than straightforward murder, although when the police were called it was discovered that

only £2 was missing from the cash register in the hotel bar, together with a few packs of cigarettes. Put like that, it was hardly the crime of the century – and nor were those responsible for the theft at all impressive in the way they had gone about committing or concealing it. Consequently it took the police barely a day to get both Gilbert and Grant into custody. Both were themselves hotel porters, and with Gilbert a former employee of the Aban Court he was certain to come under suspicion sooner rather than later. Grant did not help matters either, boasting to a colleague that he had stolen some cigarettes from another hotel the previous night and – even more bizarrely – admitting to having 'done a man in' when the evening papers ran a story about the discovery of Smart's body. Asked to collect the cigarettes from Grant's hiding place, the colleague decided to report him to the police instead and told them where the cigarettes could be found.

When they were questioned about all this, the pair naturally denied they had had any intention of killing the night porter, and both claimed to have been shocked to hear of his death. They confirmed that they had attacked him, however, 22-year-old Gilbert mentioning 'a light blow to the stomach' and 24-year-old Grant admitting he had punched Smart twice on the jaw. Grant had also stuffed a napkin into the victim's mouth while gagging him with a bandage, although, like Gilbert, he attempted to shift the blame for the death onto his accomplice.

In court the defence had hoped to secure a conviction for manslaughter, and in retrospect it does seem likely that – stupidly ill-conceived though the crime was – there was no intention beforehand to murder the older man for a couple of pounds and some smokes. But, summing up, Mr Justice Glyn-Jones made clear his opinion that the case was indeed one of murder, and that he agreed with the prosecuting barrister. Even had they not intended to kill or cause serious harm, the fact that either of the men might have contemplated violence to expedite a robbery was sufficient to make the pair of them murderers.

Thus were the fates of Gilbert and Grant sealed, the jury returning from a brief deliberation in no doubt that both men were guilty. The two immediately appealed against this judgement, but their appeals were quickly turned down by the Lord Chief Justice of England and Wales, Lord Goddard, and the death sentences allowed to stand. Lord Goddard once famously dismissed six appeals in under an hour, and in all likelihood a different defence might have produced a different result, but with each man intent on accusing the other, the end result was inevitable. On 17 June 1954 Britain's last side-by-side execution was carried out at Pentonville under the supervision of Albert Pierrepoint, with the help of Royston Rickard, Harry Smith and Joe Broadbent – that is, three assistants instead of the usual one.

GÜNTHER PODOLA -
THE LAST HANGED POLICE KILLER (1959)

⬥ **105 ONSLOW SQUARE, SW7**
⬥ **95 QUEEN'S GATE, SW7**

A TIMELY CHANGE IN THE LAW meant that Harry Roberts (p.248) was lucky enough to become the first convicted police killer to escape the noose. Günther Fritz Erwin Podola had no such luck, and instead became the last man in Britain to be sent to the gallows for much the same crime.

Born in Berlin in 1929, and later an enthusiastic member of the Hitler Youth, Podola arrived in London at the age of 30, having already served two jail terms in Canada for theft and burglary. Unskilled, unemployed and moving from one seedy Kensington hotel to another, he had come to the attention of the police within a few short months, following a burglary at an address in Roland Gardens. The tip-off came from the victim, a Mrs Verne Schiffman, who said that Podola was attempting to blackmail her by claiming to have discovered something incriminating while burgling her flat. She knew he was lying and that there was nothing in the flat to incriminate her, but knowing he would call back she alerted the police and they began monitoring her telephone line.

On 13 July Mrs Schiffman received a call that was traced by police to a telephone box at South Kensington Underground station. Detective Sergeants Purdy and Sandford were quickly in attendance and

ONSLOW SQUARE

QUEEN'S GATE

apprehended Podola on the spot. But on the way to their vehicle the latter made a break for it, running into a house at 105 Onslow Square and concealing himself behind a pillar in the hall. When Purdy entered the building he was shot dead, and Podola escaped.

IT WASN'T ME, BUT SOMEONE WHO LOOKED LIKE ME

Three days later, with police making enquiries all over the area, Podola was traced to a hotel at 95 Queen's Gate. Police broke in to a room that had been identified as belonging to the gunman, and finally emerged with their prisoner sporting a bruised face and a very obvious black eye. A search of the premises uncovered an automatic weapon concealed in the attic of the hotel. At the time, the official story was that Podola had been struck on the head by his bedroom door as it was knocked off its hinges, although the popular suspicion was that Purdy's colleagues had had a hand in his injuries. Either way Podola seemed to be in shock, and was said to be exhibiting signs of amnesia when he was examined at St Stephen's Hospital in the Fulham Road.

On 18 July at the Old Bailey, the defence, led by Mr Frederick Lawton KC, attempted to demonstrate that a series of fainting fits and memory loss rendered their client unfit to plead. It was also argued that Podola's amnesia was the direct result of injuries sustained during his second arrest – and that he was unable to recall with any clarity the events of the previous few days. Unfortunately for Podola, the jury decided against this, and the trial was reset for the next day with the same judge, Mr. Justice Edmund Davies, but a new jury.

On the 19th Podola's brief stated that, as he had been unable to obtain new instructions from his client, he would be able to do no more than to test the evidence of the other side. To this end he suggested that the killing was inadvertent, and that the gun might have been discharged accidentally while being entrusted to DS Purdy's care. This was denied by an expert from the Metropolitan Police Forensic Laboratory, and after 35 minutes the jury returned to the courtroom to pronounce Günther Podola guilty of capital murder. He was sentenced to death but still made no appeal, leaving it to the Home Secretary to refer the case on the grounds of his possible unfitness to plead.

On 15 October the Court of Criminal Appeal requested an examination be made of Podola's mental state, after which a medical tribunal met to agree that his amnesia had almost certainly been faked. This judgement was verified shortly afterwards, with Podola suddenly 'remembering' that, now he thought about it, he had actually been busily engaged burgling another property at the time of the murder, so it must have been committed by his double . . . This story failed to persuade the Court of Criminal Appeal, however, which found the trial to have been fair and just. Günther Podola was hanged at Wandsworth and buried within the prison walls.

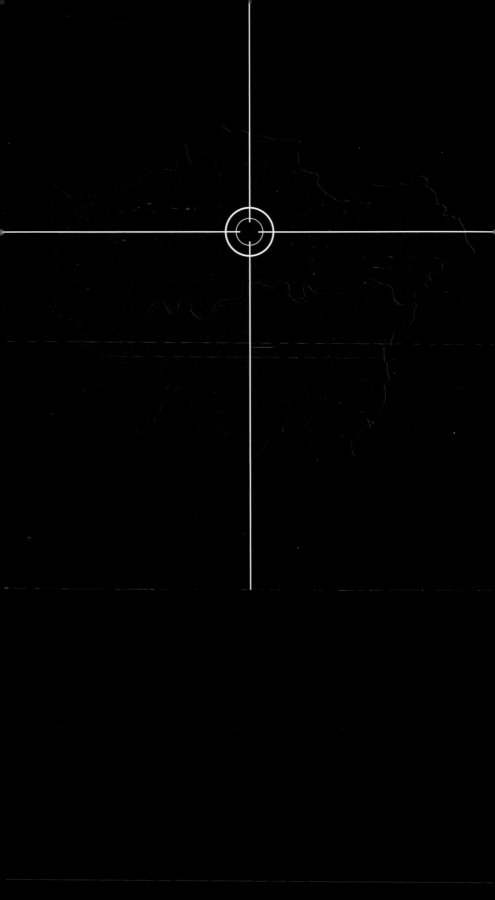

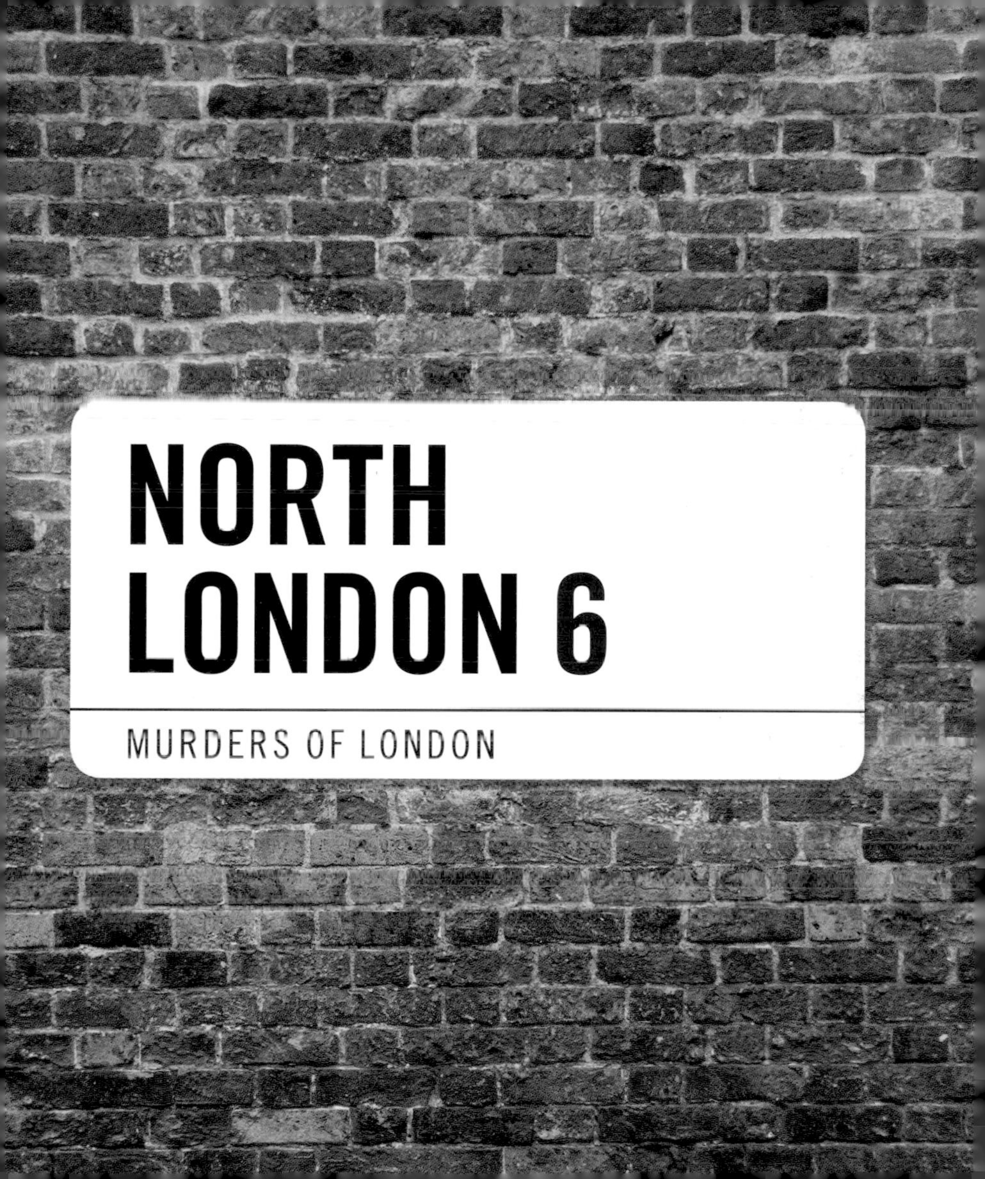
NORTH
LONDON 6
MURDERS OF LONDON

THE FINANCIAL ADVISOR
WHO WAS NOT TO BE TRUSTED
(1911)

A LAPSED FREEMASON who laboured long hours to support his large family or possibly just a greedy schemer for whom the acquisition of wealth trumped all moral considerations, Henry Seddon was a superintendent of collectors for a large industrial insurance company and also sold second-hand clothes from a shop at 276 Seven Sisters Road.

By 1910, aged 40, Seddon was also something of a small-time property speculator, buying and selling places whenever he could and renting out a four-room flat within the family's large house in Upper Holloway. His tenant that summer was the unfortunate Eliza Mary Barrow, a spinster nearly 10 years his senior who had a reasonable investment portfolio of her own, the income from which she used to look after the orphaned son and daughter of a previous landlord.

Over a period of some months, Seddon managed to inveigle his way into the spinster's inner circle, manoeuvring himself into the position of her unpaid financial adviser while using the opportunity to extract whatever he could for himself. Before very long he had offered to forego the rent and provide her with a modest annuity, in return for which she would transfer into his name £1,500 of India Stock – equivalent today to around £110,000 – or nearly 40% of her net worth. The following year he raised

her annuity to £3 a week (£220 today), whereupon the lease on the Buck's Head pub in Camden High Street moved from her portfolio into his, along with an adjoining barber's shop. Shortly after this he advised her to entrust to his care several hundred pounds from her savings account, a move he said would insulate her from the supposed long-term effects of Lloyd George's controversial 1909 budget.

IT IS MAD FOR US
TO BARROW YOUR SAVINGS

In August 1910 the Seddons – husband, wife, five children and an elderly father – took a break at Southend-on-Sea. Miss Barrow accompanied the family and brought with her the young boy who had been left in her care. But upon returning home she was suddenly taken ill and took to her bed suffering repeated bouts of diarrhoea and vomiting. Within two weeks she was dead and buried, Seddon as her executor opting for the briefest funeral and the cheapest interment – and possibly even accepting a percentage from the undertaker for introducing a new client.

On the understanding that he was now expected to look after two more children, Seddon wasted little time in taking over Barrow's remaining investments – the better, he claimed, to discharge his responsibilities as their new legal guardian. It was this final move on the part of the avaricious Seddon that was to prove his downfall.

Miss Barrows had some family, namely the Vonderahes of nearby Evershot Road. Keen to discover what had become of their dead cousin's estate, and quite possibly hoping to inherit it, they found Seddon unhelpful and obstructive. Sensing foul play, the Vonderahes requested an exhumation and post-mortem, which mostly confirmed that it was a death by natural causes but for slight traces of arsenic.

These threw the spotlight back onto Seddon, although there was of course no evidence to suggest that he or an accomplice had administered the poison. He was brought to trial, however, during which it emerged that one of the Seddon children had been sent out to buy some flypapers, which, it was noted, would be sufficient to procure a lethal dose of arsenic if boiled. This was no more than circumstantial evidence, but it didn't look good for Seddon, who had clearly profited from his association with the victim and looked set to continue doing so following her death.

In response Seddon argued, somewhat optimistically, that Barrows might accidentally have drunk the water in which the papers were dipped, while his barrister attempted to undermine the authority of the post-mortem findings. During cross-examination, Seddon's arrogant demeanour played badly with the jury, and a guilty verdict was brought in.

At this point the accused made one last extraordinary appeal for mercy to the judge, whom he had identified as a fellow Mason. Acknowledging his appeal and speaking with some emotion, Mr Justice Bicknell responded by telling Seddon, 'It is not for me to harrow your feelings – try to make peace with your Maker. We both belong to the same Brotherhood, and though that can have no influence with me this is painful beyond words to have to say what I am saying, but our Brotherhood does not encourage crime, it condemns it.' Seddon was duly hanged at Pentonville on 18 April 1912.

HAWLEY HARVEY CRIPPEN
AND THE CLASSIC ENGLISH MURDER (1910)

● **39 HILLDROP CRESCENT, N7**
● **30 CONSTANTINE ROAD, NW3**

POOR OLD DR CRIPPEN KILLED ONLY ONCE but his crime remains one of the most notorious in London's long history, and his sinister-sounding name rarely fails to get top billing in books on the history of English murder.

It helps that his tale is a classic love triangle with some low-level glamour thrown in for good measure – his wife was an amateur music hall artiste – as well as a spot of cross-dressing. The individuals involved are all characters we can recognise: the joyless, bossy and domineering wife; a henpecked husband who, against all odds, dares to take a lover; and the exotically named mistress who, to the husband's great delight, is happy to take him on. Add to this the thrilling cat-and-mouse aspect of the chase, with Scotland Yard officers using the latest technology to apprehend the suspect on the other side of the Atlantic, and the story has all the hallmarks of a Hollywood blockbuster.

Crippen's American qualification in homeopathy entitled him to call himself 'doctor' but not to practise when he arrived in Britain from Michigan in 1900. Instead he took to selling patent cures from an address in New Oxford Street, returning home to Hilldrop Crescent each evening to do the housework, as dictated by his bullying, overbearing wife.

to Scotland Yard. Dew quickly booked a passage on a much faster vessel, the *Laurentic*, and so was able to apprehend both fugitives when they stepped ashore at Quebec.

During Crippen's week at sea his notoriety had grown considerably. Captain Kendall had used the joyous wonder of wireless to keep the press informed about the lovers' movements, complete with tempting titbits about their behaviour and their personal effects. This of course did much to set the tone for the case, the two attempting to live a life of blameless domesticity behind the quiet, genteel façade of no.39 – knowing all the while that the rotting corpse of the victim lay beneath their feet.

Apparently quite relieved to have his untenable charade put an end to, Crippen made no attempt to deny his part in the murder of his wife. He was hanged at Pentonville on 23 November. Le Neve was subsequently acquitted as an accessory, and she lived on until 1967. Unfortunately no.39 and its neighbours were destroyed by enemy action in the 1940s (and later replaced by a block of flats named after Margaret Bondfield MP), but Le Neve's previous digs at 30 Constantine Road still survive.

A SERIAL HUSBAND, AND MURDERER (1915)

JUST BEFORE CHRISTMAS 1914, the *News of the World* carried the tragic story of newly married Margaret Lloyd (née Lofty), who had been found drowned in her bath in what was at the time called Bismarck Road in Highgate – renamed Waterlow Road after the war with Germany. The report attracted the attention of Mr Charles Burnham, whose daughter Alice had died in a similar fashion a year earlier, shortly after marrying George Joseph Smith against her parents' wishes.

Charles Burnham had never liked Smith, and was not convinced of the supposed manner of his daughter's death. This new report in the newspaper seemed to bear out his belief that there was something more to what he saw as his erstwhile son-in-law's 'very evil appearance'. His unease was shared by Joseph Crossley of Blackpool, Alice's landlord at the time of her death, who wrote to Detective Inspector Arthur Neil in London expressing his concerns about the parallels between the deaths of Alice and Margaret. On both occasions the bereaved husband had hastily skipped town after the most perfunctory of funerals, at one of them even telling the undertaker, 'I don't want any walking; get it over as quick as you can.'

Detective Inspector Neil thought these similarities worth investigating, not least because it seemed impossible to him that an adult could accidentally drown in as small a bath as he found at Highgate. It soon emerged that the

former Miss Lofty had emptied her Post Office account on the very day she had died, and visited a local solicitor to make a will naming her new husband as the sole beneficiary.

Neil bided his time, however, until the coroner's office informed him that a communication had been received from a life insurance firm asking for details about Margaret's death. Her life had been insured for the handsome sum of £700 – nearly a quarter of a million today, allowing for the inflation of earnings. After a short delay Neil asked the coroner to file a report suggesting that the death was not suspicious, and arrangements were made to keep watch on the solicitor's office. When 'Mr Lloyd' arrived on 1 February to collect what was due to him, the police moved in. Having ascertained that he was both John Lloyd and George Joseph Smith they arrested him, initially on a charge of bigamy.

Meanwhile newspaper reports about these so-called 'Brides in the Bath' murders had suggested a link to yet another death, dating back to July 1912. On that occasion Bessie Williams was found drowned in her bath in Herne Bay, and once again her will had only recently been changed, leaving the enormous sum of £2,579 to her new husband. Calling himself Henry Williams on that occasion, Smith had been questioned about the death but allowed to walk free when a medical report concluded that Bessie had suffered a fit in the bath.

The resemblances between the three deaths were too strong to ignore, however. Indeed, much of the significance of these murders is that they represent one of the first occasions in the history of forensic pathology and detection that similarities between different crimes were used to build a case against the defendant. The technique went on to be used in countless subsequent prosecutions, and it proved devastatingly effective in stopping George Joseph Smith.

In time more information came to light about Smith, who had pursued a criminal career from his earliest days in Bethnal Green's Roman Road. By the age of 25 he had been imprisoned three times for theft. Married once legally, in 1898, he had since gone on to marry no fewer than eight other women bigamously, on each occasion fleeing after robbing them of what money they possessed and – where necessary – killing them to collect life insurance or whatever was left him in their wills.

'I DON'T WANT ANY WALKING; GET IT OVER AS QUICK AS YOU CAN'

Finally brought to the Old Bailey on June 22 and charged with all three murders, Smith was told by the presiding judge, Mr Justice Scrutton, that he was so callous that 'an exhortation to repentance would be wasted on you.' The jury took just 20 minutes to find him guilty, and he was hanged at Maidstone Gaol on 13 August.

JOE MEEK – POP'S OWN SPACE-AGE PIONEER (1967)

304 HOLLOWAY ROAD, N7

FEW MURDERERS HAVE THEIR OWN, entirely respectable appreciation society, but influential music producer Robert George Meek, described as the 'alchemist of pop' and (wholly without irony) 'Britain's Phil Spector', was always destined to stand out from the crowd.

Meek's cramped, chaotic flat in this busy but shabby stretch of North London was where he lived, worked and died. Having soundproofed the place as best he could with only limited means, he went on to make his name with The Tornados and 'Telstar', which in 1963 was the first single by a British group to top the charts in the USA and was subsequently chosen by Lady Thatcher as one of her *Desert Island Discs*.

A friend of Brian Epstein's, and like him living very much on the wrong side of the law before the impact of the 1957 Wolfenden report, Meek famously turned down the opportunity to work with the Beatles, preferring instead to plough his own furrow. He had previously worked as an engineer for the Midlands Electricity Board, but with financial backing from the improbably named Major Wilfred Alonzo Banks he struck out to become one of this country's first independent record producers. He proved himself to be a highly eccentric innovator and a pioneer of space-age pop. During recordings, Meek would place musicians wherever he

JOE MEEK
RECORD PRODUCER
"THE TELSTAR MAN"
1929 — 1967
PIONEER OF SOUND
RECORDING TECHNOLOGY
LIVED, WORKED AND
DIED HERE

could find space for them in the flat, treating the studio itself as an instrument and frequently dismantling electrical equipment to see what he could do with it. He would play tapes backwards to create weird sounds that no-one else had yet thought of. Author and fan Jake Arnott later memorialised him as the man whose mad genius 'transformed cheap pop music into something wildly expressionistic and strangely ethereal'.

Huge hits followed as a result of Meek's uninhibited explorations, but he was clearly already a troubled individual. Raised as a girl for his first four years by a mother who had always wanted a daughter and dismissed as a sissy once he started school, his persecution complex was perhaps understandable but sat dangerously with a growing interest in the occult. According to friends, he would frequent graveyards and attempt to record the voices of the dead, and he claimed to be in touch with the spirit of his hero Buddy Holly. At other times he insisted that Decca Records were bugging his flat in order to steal his ideas.

By August 1966 Meek had money worries, too, his style of music gradually pushed to the background by the blistering success of Dylan's *Blonde on Blonde*, which was released on the 12th, and the Beatles' *Revolver*. Worse still, while one new Meek production was dismissed by reviewers as 'a whistleable little melody of promise . . . good of its kind and doubtless a hit three years ago, but not for today's market', copyright difficulties over another threatened to push him into bankruptcy.

Things worsened over the winter, particularly after the discovery on 16 January 1967 of a mutilated male body dumped in two suitcases in a field near Tattingstone, Suffolk. Meek was convinced he would be implicated in the death – although there is no evidence that he had anything to do with it – and his behaviour became increasingly erratic when the victim was identified as a teenager who was said to have hung around the studio at no. 304.

Meek increasingly displayed many of the symptoms of someone suffering from an amphetamine-induced psychosis, presumably not helped by another of his records being written off by a reviewer as 'a corny bit of beat', and it was not long until events came to a head. Dressed in black he burst in on a group of friends telling them he was possessed; the following morning, after fatally wounding his landlady, Violet Shenton, Meek turned the shotgun on himself.

The date was 3 February 1967, the eighth anniversary of Buddy Holly's death in a plane crash and a coincidence that is lost on no-one who follows the arc of Meek's career. Perhaps even more remarkable, however, is the final morbid parallel with the life of Phil Spector, another wayward recording genius with a gun, who was convicted of having murdered actress Lana Clarkson on the same date in 2003.

JOE ORTON AND KENNETH HALLIWELL
– THE DARK SIDE OF SUCCESS (1967)

ON 9 AUGUST 1967, A CHAUFFEUR ARRIVED at this top-floor flat in Noel Road to take the celebrated playwright Joe Orton to a script meeting at Twickenham Studios. After ringing and failing to get an answer, he peered through the letterbox. He was surprised to see the lights still on – it was nearly midday – and doubtless even more surprised to see the naked, bloodied body of a man lying on the hall floor.

The body belonged to 40-year-old Kenneth Halliwell, Orton's partner of more than 15 years. The two had met at RADA in the 1950s, after which both had sought to take on literary London, despite – or more probably in the face of – a teacher's assessment of the schoolboy Orton as an 11-plus failure who was merely 'semi-literate'. Halliwell's early years seem to have been slightly better spent – he had taken a Higher Schools Certificate – but for both the early years had their ups and downs, including menial jobs, periods of poverty and a spell in separate gaols for defacing many hundreds of library books.

Both had ambition, but success came first to Orton with his 1964 play *Entertaining Mr Sloane*. This and *Loot* two years later badly upset the partnership of equals that had for years existed between the pair. With an unproduced play and half a dozen unpublished novels to his name,

HISTORIC HOUSE
JOHN
KINGSLEY ORTON
(JOE ORTON)
1933 – 1967
PLAYWRIGHT
LIVED HERE
1960 – 1967
LONDON BOROUGH OF ISLINGTON

Halliwell's growing sense of failure coincided perfectly with Orton's new-found celebrity. In January 1967 Orton's diary described a meeting with Paul McCartney – he was in talks about writing a screenplay for a new Beatles film – and it was rapidly becoming apparent that, while the establishment might be happy to accommodate Orton's homosexuality, Halliwell was not well suited to play the role of writer's wife.

Fast forward a few months, and a quick look around the Noel Road flat on that August morning uncovered another body in the bedroom. This was Orton himself, although horrific injuries to the face meant that the 34-year-old was eventually identified only by a tattoo of a bird over an old appendectomy scar. He had been battered to death in nine hammer-blows by the blood-spattered Halliday, who in turn had then washed down nearly two dozen Nembutal tablets with a can of grapefruit juice before collapsing in the hall. Autopsies revealed that Halliday had actually died first.

'IF YOU READ THIS DIARY ALL WILL BE EXPLAINED'

Halliwell's motive was confirmed by a suicide note found close to Orton's journal, which advised the reader: 'If you read this diary all will be explained – K.H. PS. Especially the latter parts.' Clearly, as Orton's star had risen, the balance of the relationship had tipped irreversibly. Halliwell was intensely envious of Orton's success and frustrated by his own lack of it. Orton may well have felt himself under pressure to break off the relationship, and it was certainly clear from his diary that he was enjoying flaunting his new fame and a more promiscuous lifestyle in a manner that badly upset Halliwell.

Already concerned that he was being eased out of Orton's life, Halliwell must have read with horror diary entries describing their rows – 'exhausting wrangles over trivia' – and observing how he, Orton, was shining in company whereas Halliwell was increasingly just aggressive, withdrawn and rude to his boyfriend's famous friends. The diaries also provided proof that Orton no longer found the physical side of their relationship at all fulfilling. Entry after entry reveals a casual approach to infidelity, with Orton seeking satisfaction all over North London. One entry in particular described in detail a veritable orgy in a public lavatory on the Holloway Road, exactly the kind of encounter Halliwell could not stand.

In the decades since his death it has often been observed that the macabre circumstances of Orton's demise could well have found a place in one of his own dark comedies. Certainly, reading his diary, Halliwell might well have drawn a horrifying connection between his own life and Orton's depictions of such appetites as lust and greed to spotlight the bleak emptiness and essential loneliness of human existence. But according to friends the playwright would never have left Halliwell, despite their rows, the furious demands for Orton to control his taste for casual sex, and Halliwell's obvious jealousy.

The two men were cremated at Golders Green and their ashes mingled and buried together. Today a plaque marks the house in this quiet, sunlit street.

DENNIS NILSEN,
THE LONELY SERIAL
KILLER (1983)

● **23 CRANLEY GARDENS, N10**
● **195 MELROSE AVENUE, NW2**

DENNIS NILSEN, A FORMER ARMY CHEF and trainee police constable who had settled down to a superficially unremarkable life as a junior clerk in the Civil Service, succeeded in killing and concealing more victims than would seem plausible in a city as densely populated as late-twentieth-century London. At the same time one could argue that his crimes could have happened nowhere else.

The part of Nilsen's story with which we are concerned begins in the late 1970s, when he moved to 195 Melrose Avenue, Cricklewood, with Bleep, a one-eyed mongrel. A heavy-drinking homosexual, Nilsen met Stephen Holmes in the Cricklewood Arms on 30 December 1978 and took him home, later strangling him with a necktie and then dunking his head into a bucket of water. He concealed the corpse under the floorboards for eight months until the smell drove him to incinerate it on a bonfire in the back garden.

With a little variation this was a pattern he went on to repeat eleven times over the next three years, interring each victim under the floorboards and only later burning the remains on local waste ground when the smell became too awful. On two occasions the would-be victims

CRANLEY GARDENS

MELROSE AVENUE

escaped, and Nilsen was almost caught. But one declined to press charges and the police dismissed the other as a lovers' tiff.

The truth is that, intentionally or not, Nilsen selected his victims well, alighting on marginal homosexuals drifting amid an anonymous population – individuals, in other words, who were unlikely to be reported missing or to arouse suspicion by not turning up for work. Consequently, when Nilsen moved out in 1981, he seemed to have got away with it – and might indeed have done so had his murderous drive not travelled with him from Cricklewood to what was then a rather seedy and dilapidated part of Muswell Hill.

'I WAS DESPERATE FOR COMPANY, EVEN IF IT WAS ONLY A BODY'

At Cranley Gardens Nilsen and Bleep found themselves living in a top-floor flat, meaning that no more corpses could be stored beneath the floorboards. Before long, however, Nilsen had devised a solution: he continued to strangle or drown his victims, but now he took to dismembering the corpses and cooking up the remains before disposing of them piecemeal. Some body parts were flushed down the lavatory, others rendered on the kitchen stove, and some simply left out in black bin bags for the dustmen to cart away. Three more victims disappeared this way – all strangers whom Nilsen befriended in West End pubs – before his fellow tenants began to complain about the blocked drains

The law finally caught up with Nilsen on 7 February 1983, after a plumbing company confirmed that the drains were clogged with human remains. When arresting officers tentatively asked whether he had killed one or two people, Nilsen – visibly relieved at being arrested at last – astonished them by replying, 'Fifteen or sixteen'. He directed the police to two plastic bags in his wardrobe, which contained more human remains. Once detectives had retraced Nilsen's steps back to Cricklewood and started digging around in Melrose Avenue, a defence of 'diminished responsibility' seemed most likely.

In lay terms, Nilsen's actions were certainly those of a madman, and his defence team must have hoped to bring in a verdict of manslaughter rather than murder. But in the event they were unsuccessful. On 4 November 1983, three weeks before his 38th birthday, Dennis Andrew Nilsen was convicted at the Old Bailey of six murders and two attempted murders after twelve hours of deliberation. The judge recommended a minimum of 25 years, later raised to a whole life tariff. Bleep spent his remaining days at Battersea Dogs' Home.

It took until 2005 for Stephen Holmes to be positively identified, and, nearly three decades after Nilsen's conviction, seven of the 15 victims are still unknown – a sad reflection on the short, chaotic and disconnected lives they must have led. Nilsen claimed he was merely 'desperate for company, even if it was only a body', but his motives are even now not really clear at all.

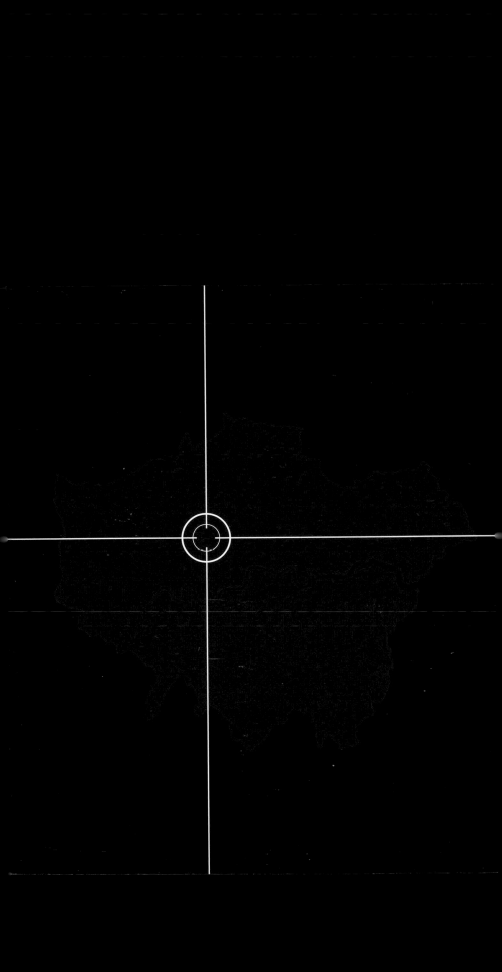

NORTH WEST LONDON 7

MURDERS OF LONDON

THE CAMDEN TOWN
MURDER (1907)

THAT THE SO-CALLED CAMDEN TOWN MURDER – the violent and bloody death of Phyllis Dimmock – remains unsolved has caused comparisons to be drawn between it and the activities of Jack the Ripper in Whitechapel (p.22), even though the two are separated by several miles and a good two decades.

In 1907 Phyllis, a Hertfordshire publican's daughter, was renting digs with her partner in what was then St Paul's Road and is now Agar Grove. She styled herself 'Mrs Bertram Shaw', although there is no evidence to suggest that the two were ever legally married. Mr Shaw was employed as a cook on one of the overnight services of the Midland Railway, so Dimmock filled the long hours of his absence by working locally as a prostitute. Favourite pick-ups were The Rising Sun (now The Rocket) at 120 Euston Road and The Old Eagle in Royal College Street, and it was her habit to entertain clients a few minutes' walk away at home.

Dimmock is known to have visited both pubs prior to her husband's return from Derby on the morning of 12 September. He found her naked and mutilated corpse on the floor of their flat, her throat cut from ear to ear, and the flat had been ransacked. The time of death was estimated as somewhere in the early hours.

investigations soon revealed that, on three of the preceding four evenings, the deceased had been at The Rising Sun with another cook called Robert Roberts. Also that she had excused herself on the fourth occasion by showing him a postcard suggesting she had a prior engagement and was unable to meet him. Roberts, it quickly transpired, had a reliable alibi for the night of 11 September, so the postcard – discovered at no.29 – seemed to offer the best chance of catching the murderer.

Instead of naming the designated rendezvous, the card included a little sketch showing a cheerful sun rising over the horizon and winking broadly at the reader. It was signed 'Alice', but when it was published in the *News of the World* the style and handwriting caught the eye of another prostitute, Ruby Young, who fingered a former boyfriend and graphic artist named Robert Wood.

Wood was soon charged with murder and hauled into court, where, by very great fortune, he was to be defended by one of the great advocates of his age, the aforementioned Sir Edward Marshall Hall (p.90). Wood himself, however, was a shockingly bad witness. Striking a self-consciously superior pose, he refused to answer even the most straightforward questions from his own counsel, such as, 'Mr Wood, did you kill Emily Dimmock?' On being asked the same question a second time, Wood affected to find it ridiculous, leading some to suggest that his juvenile posturing might have been sufficient to persuade the jury that he was incapable of committing such a crime.

A more likely explanation for his acquittal is that Sir Edward won the day for him, as his performance in the case won him the nickname 'the Great Defender'. Either way it took the jury just 15 minutes to find Wood not guilty.

With no other evidence to direct them, the police moved on and the public gradually lost interest. As a consequence Dimmock might not even be remembered today, were it not for the spurious 'Ripper' connection and a controversial attempt to cash in on the publicity surrounding the case by the German-born Impressionist Walter Sickert.

Sickert had for some years been painting ordinary domestic interiors, as part of which he had produced a number of works depicting sombre, reflective-looking nudes lying on beds. Following the trial of Robert Wood he exhibited a group of four such paintings under the collective title *The Camden Town Murder*, including one showing a man staring down at the floor with the lifeless figure of a naked woman immediately behind him. The resulting controversy certainly succeeded in raising his artistic profile, and today the four paintings number among Sickert's best-known works.

'WHAT SHALL WE DO TO PAY THE RENT?'

The exhibition proved controversial in more ways than one, however, since a number of recent books have suggested Sickert himself was Phyllis Dimmock's killer – some go so far as to speculate that he was in fact the Ripper. That Sickert, like Roberts, could produce alibis seems no longer to matter, and neither does it matter that the paintings had previously appeared with entirely different titles. One was simply called *Summer Afternoon* and the one with the man in it *What Shall We Do to Pay the Rent?*, which puts a very different spin on the image but has done little to rescue Sickert's posthumous reputation.

ALLAN CHAPPELOW
FOUND BATTERED
TO DEATH (2006)

THE MANOR, 9 DOWNSHIRE HILL, NW3

BORN IN COPENHAGEN BUT RAISED IN LONDON, author and photographer Allan Chappelow moved to Downshire Hill as a boy and – aside from a few years at boarding school and at Cambridge – he lived here until his 86-year-old body was found battered and bloodied under piles of personal papers in 2006.

Chappelow had been one of the first Western tourists to visit the USSR after World War II, and had briefly worked as a photographer for the *Daily Mail* and *Daily Telegraph* in the 1950s. Latterly something of a recluse, today his reputation relies on two volumes of biography of George Bernard Shaw, with whom he formed a notable friendship.

Having lived at The Manor for the best part of three-quarters of a century, Chappelow cut a familiar if eccentric figure around Hampstead, reportedly refusing to have a telephone in the house and making his rare forays to the local library astride a 1940s motorbike. According to neighbours, and regardless of the weather, Chappelow would make these excursions dressed in a leather helmet with an old mac tied shut with a length of string. 'Never very domestically inclined', according to one neighbour, Chappelow also made attempts to repair the Georgian property himself, using plastic bags in place of missing roof slates and securing loose guttering with sticky tape.

In June 2006, the police were notified by Chappelow's bank that there had been a series of suspicious transactions involving one of his accounts but that the old man himself appeared to be uncontactable. They arrived at the house to find the front garden heavily overgrown and the path blocked by vegetation and an assortment of junk. Inside, they found Chappelow's body covered in wax and burns and buried under a 3-foot pile of papers. Blood was spattered a metre and a half up the walls.

A FAMILIAR IF ECCENTRIC FIGURE AROUND HAMPSTEAD

Evidence that Chappelow's post had been tampered with seemed to indicate that he was a victim of identity theft, but it subsequently proved impossible to date his killing with any accuracy. In October, however, police announced that a suspect had been arrested in Switzerland, and a 43-year-old financial trader was subsequently extradited and charged with battering the author to death, stealing his identity and raiding his bank accounts.

As far as a motive was concerned, the accused was known to have money difficulties: he had been declared bankrupt and been facing eviction from a property in a neighbouring street since 2004. But in early 2007 the case took an unexpected turn when the *Evening Standard* reported that Home Secretary Jacqui Smith was seeking to have part of the trial held in secret on the grounds of national security. The defendant, the Old Bailey was told, had been one of the leaders of the 1989 Tiananmen Square uprising and part of his defence was expected to involve his work for MI6. On 14 January 2008 the necessary gagging order was granted, an unprecedented move in a case involving murder, burglary and deception.

On 31 March the case reached its conclusion and the defendant was convicted by an 11-1 majority of obtaining a £20,000 money transfer by deception and of stealing £20 from a cash machine. The following day the jury found the same individual also guilty of handling stolen goods in relation to a mobile phone, four blank cheques and cash. Thereafter, in the absence of any reliable forensic evidence, and unable to reach verdicts in relation to charges of murder or burglary, they were discharged by the trial judge, Mr Justice Ouseley.

A retrial in October saw the case for the prosecution held in public but that for the defence 'in camera'. The prosecution took eight weeks telling its side of the story, producing CCTV evidence of a credit card in Chappelow's name being used at the Curry Paradise restaurant in South End Green. Once again the most serious charge was denied, but in his summing up Judge Ouseley told the jury that the Crown's case 'essentially found that the person who stole Mr Chappelow's identity was the same person responsible for the killing'.

On 16 January 2009 the BBC reported that the former dissident – still being granted anonymity and still insisting he was framed by 'men with no allegiance to this country' – had been convicted of Chappelow's murder and sentenced to 20 years. More recently, permission has been granted for the listed but dilapidated Manor House to be dismantled and the site developed.

A DANGEROUS MAN
WITH A CHIP ON HIS SHOULDER (1949)

620B FINCHLEY ROAD, NW11

ON 21 OCTOBER 1949 A PUNT-GUNNER out after ducks near Tillingham in the Essex marshes chanced upon a waterlogged package. Upon being opened, this turned out to contain a headless, legless human torso with five stab wounds visible on the chest.

An examination by the Home Office pathologist Prof. Francis Camps indicated that the stab wounds accounted for the victim's death, and the large number of broken bones suggested to Camps that the body may have been dropped from a substantial height. Although the remains had been in the water for some while, the police were able to get prints from the victim's fingers and these matched a set they already had on file for a 44-year-old Baghdadi called Stanley Setty. A used-car dealer of decidedly questionable character, Setty was quite far from his usual London patch, and the police soon discovered that he had gone missing more than two weeks previously, together with £1,000 in five pound notes.

While the serial numbers of the missing notes were circulated to the press, the police, acting on a hunch that the body might have been thrown from an aeroplane, started asking around local flying clubs to see if anyone had seen anything suspicious. Very soon a United Services Flying Club mechanic came up with something very useful indeed, recalling one

of his members, Brian Donald Hume, manhandling a large package into an aeroplane before taking off from Elstree on 5 October.

Tracing Hume was easy enough and he was promptly arrested at the flat above what was then a greengrocer's near Golders Green Station, which he shared with his wife and new baby. The case against him was building nicely. The mechanic's story was backed up by evidence of damage to a window of the plane, the testimony of a taxi driver who had driven Hume back to London and been paid using some of Setty's money, and bloodstains in the flat that appeared to match the victim's blood type. When he was interviewed at Albany Street Police Station, however, Hume vehemently denied any part in the murder, conceding only that he had been paid by three strangers to dump a large parcel into the sea. The three he could identify only as Mac, Greeny and The Boy, whom he said had paid him £150 to do the job and keep mum.

Hume stuck to this story when he appeared at the Old Bailey on 18 January 1950, and the foreman subsequently had to admit that the jury could not reach a verdict. A second jury was sworn in but was formally ordered to find Hume not guilty of a charge of murder, so it seemed the only charge he could be convicted on was one of being an accessory by disposing of the body.

Sentenced to 12 years but released from Broadmoor after serving just eight, Hume promptly sold his story to the *Sunday Pictorial* for £3,600, a staggering sum at the time. He used the opportunity to admit cheerfully to his six million readers that, grasping an authentic SS dagger, a wartime souvenir, 'my sweating hand plunged the weapon frenziedly and repeatedly into his chest and legs.'

He was, he said, born with a chip on his shoulder as big as an elephant, and learned as a child that, 'if you have an enemy, get rid of him.'

NORTH WEST LONDON

Unfortunately this was something he proved again within weeks of his release, shooting a bank manager during a raid in Brentford and then – after fleeing to Switzerland – killing a taxi driver after an attempt on a bank in Zurich. The latter earned him 16 years in a Swiss jail before he was sent back to Britain and returned to Broadmoor, where he was apparently a model patient. In 1998 the *Sunday Mirror* reported that the 78-year-old, now released, had been found dead in the grounds of a Basingstoke hotel, apparently of natural causes.

'I HEREBY CONFESS TO THE SUNDAY PICTORIAL THAT I STABBED HIM TO DEATH'

LONDON'S MOST FAMOUS
CRIME PASSIONNEL
(1955)

THE MAGDALA, SOUTH HILL PARK, NW3

WERE IT NOT FOR THE FACT THAT BRITAIN no longer exercises the right to hang convicted killers, the likelihood is that few of us would remember Ruth Ellis, the Welsh-born daughter of a Belgian emigrée and a roving cruise-line cellist. The premeditated murder of her lover, David Blakely, outside this Hampstead pub on Easter Sunday 1955 was certainly violent, and 30 years later it was to form the basis of an enjoyable film, *Dance With a Stranger*, starring Miranda Richardson. But in most other regards it was a fairly commonplace story, a run-of-the-mill 'domestic', in police parlance, although the press at the time dressed things up a bit after detecting a whiff of a more engaging *crime passionnel*.

Ellis was a nightclub manageress and Blakely a racing driver, albeit not a very good one. The two had been introduced to each other by Britain's first ever Formula One world champion, the sport's golden boy Mike Hawthorn, which was precisely the sort of detail that lent proceedings a much-needed touch of glamour. But the real interest in the case depends on the sentence passed down by the judge, Sir Cecil Havers – grandfather, incidentally, of *Chariots of Fire* actor Nigel – and the fact that Ellis was the last woman to be executed under English law.

Prior to the murder, the match between Ellis and Blakely had never been anything but tempestuous. Three days before the shooting they had been making love at her flat at 44 Egerton Gardens, Kensington, but the former nude model and divorced mother-of-two had taken another lover on the side. Blakely, too, was apparently playing the field, clearly besotted by Ellis but almost certainly considering her beneath him socially. When he failed to show up for a date on Good Friday, she tracked him down to Hampstead, where she watched him leave a party with a girl on his arm. Two days later, having fortified herself with a bottle of Pernod and an old .38 service revolver, Ellis waited outside the Magdala. When Blakely stepped outside she shot him dead. 'FOUR BULLETS AS HE LAY DYING' was the headline in the *Daily Mail*, and the holes one can still see in the tiled façade of this friendly Victorian pub were supposedly caused by her gun.

'IT IS OBVIOUS THAT WHEN I SHOT HIM I INTENDED TO KILL HIM'

On the basis of these brief details a sentence of death seemed assured, and one was duly handed down at the Old Bailey in June of that year. Ellis refused to appeal against the sentence, and had she done so her declaration to the prosecuting counsel, Christmas Humphreys QC – 'It is obvious that when I shot him I intended to kill him' – is likely to have undermined any attempt to do so. Her choice of weapon was also somewhat problematic: in court she insisted she had owned it for years but never used it, although a forensic examination indicated very clearly that it had been cleaned and oiled immediately before the attack.

At 9am on 13 July 1955, Ruth Ellis became the fifteenth woman to be hanged in England in the 20th century. Despite this not inconsiderable total, the idea of hanging a woman has always been seen as somehow more shocking than executing a man, and indeed the 50,000-signature petition handed to the Home Office and the large crowd assembled outside Holloway Prison at the appointed hour suggested that this was a rather more controversial case than most. Among the many who felt compelled to protest publicly was the novelist Raymond Chandler, who launched a blistering attack on the authorities in a letter to the London *Evening Standard*, describing what he called the 'medieval savagery of the law'.

Following her execution, and in line with normal practice at the time, the 29-year-old's body was buried in an unmarked grave within the prison grounds. In 1971, during rebuilding work at Holloway, permission was sought and obtained to remove her remains to St Mary's Church in Amersham – barely half a dozen miles from the Blakely family home at Penn, which is the final resting place of her erstwhile lover and victim.

Today the chief legacy of the Ellis case is that it added considerable fuel to the fire for those organisations already seeking the abolition of the death penalty in Britain. Interestingly, one of those who in time came to support this movement was the aforementioned prosecutor Christmas Humphreys, an early convert to Zen Buddhism – his former home at 58 Marlborough Place in St John's Wood is now a monastery – and who famously prosecuted not just Ellis but also Timothy Evans, Derek Bentley and Christopher Craig, and the Cold War 'atom spy' Klaus Fuchs.

ANOTHER FATAL DOMESTIC (1954)

11 SOUTH HILL PARK, NW3

BY QUITE REMARKABLE COINCIDENCE South Hill Park, infamous as the backdrop to the Ruth Ellis case (p.170), had been the scene of another fatal domestic the previous year, in which the leading player – a fiery-tempered, middle-aged Greek Cypriot – became the penultimate woman hanged for murder in Britain.

Styllou Pantopiou Christofi had arrived in London in 1953 to live with her son Stavros, a waiter, and his German wife in their ground-floor flat at no.11. By contemporary accounts Stavros and Hella's twelve-year marriage had been a happy one, but the arrival of the mother-in-law from hell soon put things under an intolerable strain. Unable to speak English at all well – and apparently unwilling to learn – the 53-year-old Mrs Christofi disliked cold, grey London, strongly disapproved of the way in which her daughter-in-law was raising her grandchildren, and lost no opportunity to pick a fight or disrupt the family's life in any way she could.

Later it emerged that she had considerable previous form here, having in her mid-20s been charged with murdering her own mother-in-law by forcing open the woman's mouth and ramming home a flaming torch. The resulting injuries must have been truly horrifying, but a Cypriot court found that Christofi had no case to answer, perhaps

concluding – who knows? – that passion and possessiveness were only to be expected from a spirited individual with such a lively Mediterranean temperament.

Unfortunately for Stavros and Hella the passing years had not caused Christofi to mellow one whit, and by 1954 Hella said she was taking the children on a trip to Germany and that Stavros should do whatever was necessary to pack his mother off back to Cyprus. Unbeknownst to Hella, her mother-in-law had also concluded that the situation was untenable, but the solution she set in train on 29 July was altogether more drastic. She first hit 36-year-old Hella over the head, and then strangled her as she lay unconscious on the kitchen floor.

A curious choice of weapon, the cast-iron ashplate from the kitchen range, was perhaps the first indication that Christofi's plan had not been especially well thought-out. The second was her decision to incinerate the body in order to get rid of the evidence – an absurdly optimistic scheme, even allowing for the primitive state of forensic science in the mid-1950s, and highly impractical in such a heavily built-up residential area.

Undeterred by common sense, Christofi dragged Hella's body out of the back of the building and doused it with paraffin. Under the watchful eye of a neighbour who was reading at a window overlooking the Christofis' garden, she dropped a match on the body and then went back into the house to tidy up. As it happens the neighbour watching all this assumed she was simply disposing of an old shop mannequin or tailor's dummy, and so felt no need to raise the alarm. But Christofi felt otherwise, and after a few minutes, with the funeral pyre well underway in the garden, she rushed out into the street to buttonhole a stranger whom she persuaded into the flat.

'Please come,' she told him in her halting English. 'Fire burning. Children sleeping.' It seemed her luck had run out at last, however, the passer-by quickly taking stock of the bizarre circumstances in which he found himself, spying the remains of a body, and deciding to call the police.

In custody Christofi immediately attempted to portray the whole thing as a ghastly accident. Besides the forensic evidence and the testimony of Stavros, who understandably refused ever to visit or speak to his mother again, her fate must have been sealed even before rumours reached London from Cyprus about her earlier arrest. Even so, it is tempting to suppose that certain details of the case – the choice of weapon, most obviously – might have enabled Christofi to mount some kind of a defence, perhaps on the grounds that it was an impetuous act in the heat of an argument. The public had little time for such theories, however, and – compared to Ruth Ellis, whose actions were clearly premeditated – there was relatively little outcry when Christofi went to the gallows on 13 December 1954.

'PLEASE COME FIRE BURNING CHILDREN SLEEPING'

That she was a foreigner almost certainly played a role here, and locally she would have been seen as something of a homewrecker or modern-day harpy. Certainly her executioner, Albert Pierrepoint, was struck by the differing reactions to the two South Hill Park crimes, noting in his memoir that it was the 'blonde night-club hostess' who won the hearts of the public – one of whom even promised him £90 if he refused to hang Ruth Ellis – rather than the 'grey-haired and bewildered grandmother who spoke no English'.

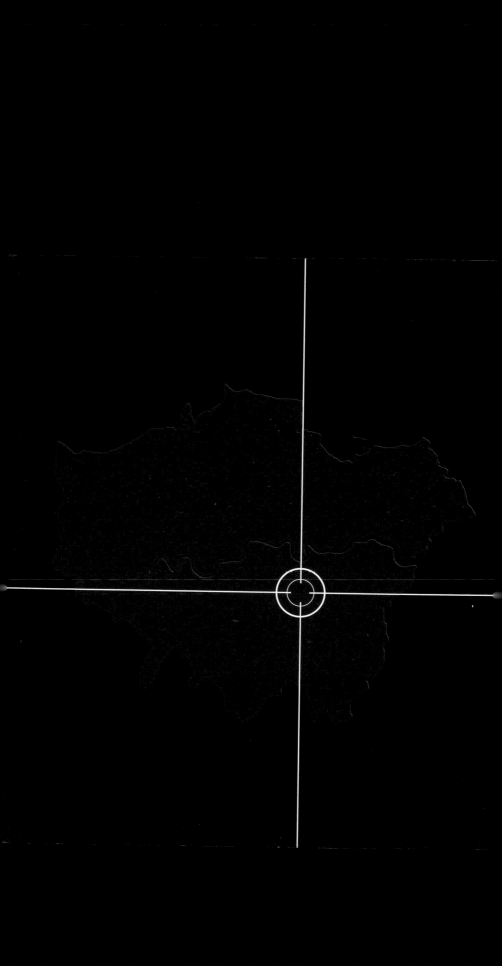

SOUTH EAST LONDON 8

MURDERS OF LONDON

WHEN YOU LIVE
BY THE SWORD...
(2003)

● **304 LYNTON ROAD, SE1**

SOUTH EAST LONDON CAN CLAIM the dubious honour of London's first ever recorded murder, that of Aelfheah or St Alphege in 1012. As Archbishop of Canterbury, Alphege was put to death by the Danes, and exactly 1,000 years later his name lives on in the dedication of the finest church in Greenwich.

George Francis lacks any such memorial, but as an associate of the Kray twins (p.30) he is perhaps equally unlikely to be forgotten. Having survived the murder and mayhem those two inflicted on East London in the 1950s and '60s and been linked in one way or another to 20 gangland killings, Francis was himself gunned down outside the yard of his haulage firm, Signed, Sealed & Delivered, in 2003.

In fact his fame, such as it is, springs from more than one source, as Francis was also implicated in another widely reported and decidedly notorious crime. This was the 1983 Brink's-Mat bullion job, an undertaking frequently ranked alongside the Great Train Robbery as an example of the kind of brilliant criminal enterprise that somehow makes heroes of those who would otherwise be dismissed as everyday London villains.

Francis's violent death on 14 May 2003 was arguably to be expected, then, and indeed the *Independent* suggested that, 'as an old-time crook and associate of such criminal luminaries as the Krays, Kenneth Noye

when he was gunned down. He was shot four times – in the face, back, arm and hand – and his death bore all the signs of a professional gangland 'hit'. The gunmen had clearly been lying in wait for their target – it was 5 a.m. – and several witnesses reporting hearing tyres squealing as the killers made their getaway.

This was the second time such an attempt had been made: in 1985 Francis had survived being shot in the chest at a pub he owned in Kent. Once again, as a police spokesman drily observed after Francis had been pronounced dead, there was 'no shortage of suspects'.

Of course, you can tell a lot about a man from the company he keeps. George Francis, who collected a total of five convictions for violence, already had a reputation as a useful hard man by the age of sixteen. In later life, he was regularly seen around town with the likes of Ronnie and Reggie Kray and the Richardsons, while guests at his daughter's wedding included at least two of the Great Train robbers, Buster Edwards and Charlie Wilson.

In 1981 Francis was cleared of involvement in a huge cannabis-smuggling racket, and two years later he watched as the swimming pool at his home in Kent was drained and dug up by police looking for the 6,800 gold bars stolen in the Brink's-Mat robbery. They were not found, but in 1986 Francis spent a year in jail for possession of forged bank notes. Shortly after his release he was in trouble again, this time collecting a 16-year sentence and a £300,000 fine for smuggling cannabis.

On being released he claimed to have gone straight, although he maintained close friendships with a number of notorious South London 'faces'. These included another member of the Brink's-Mat gang, Brian Perry, who was himself gunned down in 2002 outside a minicab firm in which he had an interest.

In 2007 two ageing hitmen, John O'Flynn and Terence Conaghan, were found guilty of killing George Francis and were jailed for a minimum of 20 years. The pair, who between them had more than 120 previous convictions, were caught after O'Flynn got drunk and started bragging about his criminal exploits to a girlfriend. Thereafter an abundance of forensic evidence – including a discarded cigarette end and lots of CCTV footage – linked both men to the scene of the crime.

At their trial at the Old Bailey it was suggested that 63-year-old Francis had been 'rubbed out' after reneging on a deal requiring him to look after £5 billion in Brink's-Mat gold. This has not been confirmed, but his was the ninth death to be linked to this one robbery. Since then, with police admitting they expected more killings as the settling of old scores continued, talk of a Brink's-Mat curse has proved hard to quash.

'THERE WAS AN INEVITABILITY THAT HE WOULD COME TO A SORRY END'

EDMUND POOK
AND THE SERVANT GIRL (1891)

- **THE MITRE, GREENWICH HIGH ROAD, SE10**
- **MORDEN COLLEGE, ST GERMAN'S PLACE, SE3**
- **KIDBROOKE LANE, SE9**

WITH IMMORAL RELATIONS BETWEEN a young master and servant, an unplanned pregnancy and a brutal killing with a hammer, the story that emerged following the discovery of a 17-year-old girl battered and bleeding to death on Eltham Common, was a gift to the sensationalist press of the 1870s.

The eventual acquittal of the only suspect in the case aroused particularly strong feelings – strong enough for a crowd of several thousand to follow a cart through the streets of Greenwich on which was mounted a grisly tableau showing the lifelike figure of 20-year-old Edmund Pook hoisting a hammer over the head of the servant girl Jane Clousen. When the cart stopped outside the Mitre, a tavern opposite what was then 3 London Street – now a Cafe Rouge – the crowd turned ugly.

Pook was employed in his father's printing business and, at the time of the murder, lived with his parents. On 13 April 1891, after two years' good service, Jane Clousen was curtly dismissed by Mrs Pook. The reason given was her slovenly habits and appearance, but Mrs Pook had sensed something developing between her son and the servant girl and wanted an end to it. Jane took lodgings a few hundred yards away in Ashburnham Place, and, already pregnant, confessed to her landlady that she and Edmund were actually engaged.

THE MITRE

MORDEN COLLEGE

KIDBROOKE LANE

There is some suggestion that the pair had secretly arranged to meet a couple of weeks after Jane's dismissal; either way, on the 27th, a policeman patrolling along Kidbrooke Lane in nearby Eltham (by the moated Tudor Barn in what is now the gardens of Well Hall Pleasaunce) came upon a severely injured girl attempting to crawl along the road. She was, he said, quietly moaning, 'Oh, my poor head, my poor head.' The girl was Jane Clousen, and she died shortly after being taken to Guy's Hospital.

MY POOR HEAD, MY POOR HEAD

The wounds to Jane's head were truly awful: a doctor's report produced at Edmund Pook's trial described their 'incised character', with cuts right down to the bone, fragments of bone 'lying quite loose' and the skull itself so badly damaged that 'the brain was discovered to be lacerated.' Further examination confirmed that she was indeed two months pregnant, although the baby was thought to have died in utero well before the attack.

The murder weapon, a distinctive plasterer's hammer, was found quite some distance away in the gardens of the seventeenth-century Morden College. It had been wiped clean but still bore traces of blood. A shopkeeper at 186 Deptford High Street confirmed that he had sold the implement to a man matching Edmund Pook's description, and another witness claimed that he had seen a figure who might have been Pook hurrying along Kidbrooke Lane the previous evening.

When he was interviewed by the police, Pook confirmed that he had seen Jane the previous evening, but that she had been in the company of another man whom he could not identify. It also emerged that Pook had not been the man who bought the hammer in Deptford. When bloodstains were found on his clothing, however, he was charged with Jane's murder.

Newspaper coverage of the trial, which commenced at the Old Bailey on 10 July, was extensive. The popular press tapped into an exceptional vein of resentment while risking a charge of libel (and even of perverting the course of justice) by depicting a scenario that most readers would have recognised. Having got a servant into trouble and not wishing to marry beneath his dignity, the young gentleman had clearly bumped her off rather than face up to his responsibilities. The jury thought otherwise, however, and Pook was quickly acquitted when no evidence of an improper relationship between him and the girl was forthcoming. With the prosecution failing to produce any correspondence to prove the two had remained in touch after Jane's dismissal, the verdict was greeted by cheers in the courtroom – and booing outside it. The large and unruly crowd that had gathered now burned with anger at what they saw as a guilty middle-class man literally getting away with murder.

As the mob would have heard none of the evidence, it seems fair to say that much of the fury and bitterness was based on hearsay and the case is often cited as one of the earliest examples of trial by media. Pook attempted to return to his normal life but, keen to whip up sales, pamphleteers continued to harass the family in the months that followed. After a couple of successful libel suits the Pooks eventually changed their names and fled the capital, but the mystery lived on. In the 1871 census the recording officer wrote one word next to the name of Jane Maria Clousen: MURDERED.

THE LAMBETH
POISONER (1891)

● **DUKE OF WELLINGTON, 81-83 WATERLOO ROAD, SE1**

ONE OF SEVERAL NAMES to be put in the frame for the Ripper killings (p.22), Thomas Neill Cream stands apart from most in that he was at least a convicted murderer who hanged for his crimes. He is also occasionally reported to have confessed, uttering the words 'I am Jack the Ri—' as the trapdoor on the gallows fell away – although none of the official witnesses to his execution claim to have heard any such thing.

Cream was nevertheless a thoroughly bad egg, a Scots-born doctor who trained at St Thomas's Hospital and then in Canada, returning across the Atlantic in 1891 to murder several London prostitutes using strychnine.

In Canada he had relished his work as an abortionist, attracting the attention of the authorities when a patient was found dead on his premises with clear symptoms of chloroform poisoning, and then two years later when a patient died on the operating table. He soon skipped town to Chicago, where he started selling various quack remedies for epilepsy, but then he killed his lover's husband after spicing up the brew with some additives of his own. When one of these turned out to be strychnine and his lover turned state's evidence, Cream managed to escape the noose once again but was sent to the Joliet Correctional Centre.

Cream subsequently returned to London, where he moved into a hotel on Fleet Street and took to frequenting the prostitutes of Lambeth and Waterloo. Perhaps to cut down on his commute, he moved to new lodgings

at 103 Lambeth Palace Road. On at least one occasion he was seen in the company of prostitute Ellen Donworth, who on 16 October was taken ill outside the Duke of Wellington pub on Waterloo Road and subsequently died, the symptoms of nausea and convulsions leading police to a diagnosis of strychnine poisoning. This theory was supported by a letter to the police – penned by Cream, though this was not yet known – suggesting that Ellen's murderer was Lt. Frederick Smith MP, later the 2nd Viscount Hambledon and the heir to the W. H. Smith & Son fortune.

For the time being, Cream was in the clear, and on the 20th he struck again, picking up 27-year-old Matilda Clover in a pub called the Canterbury Arms on Upper Marsh and going back to her digs at 27 Lambeth Road. She, too, was dead the following morning, and once again the symptoms indicated strychnine poisoning – although it took a while for her death to be considered suspicious since she was such a notorious drunk. It was not until the arrival of a second letter that the police really took notice. This time the letter was addressed to Lady Russell at the Savoy Hotel and suggested that her estranged husband was responsible for this latest killing. Another accusatory letter went to the eminent neurologist William Broadbent and was hastily forwarded to Scotland Yard as it contained a threat of blackmail.

There was still nothing to link the killings to Cream, however, and after a brief return trip across the Atlantic he was back in action again, offering a restorative capsule to a prostitute whom he had picked up in Leicester Square. Suspicious of his motives, Lou Harvey dropped the medication into the Thames, but two other working girls, Emma Shrivell and Alice Marsh, were less fortunate: they died shortly after Cream had visited them at their flat in Stamford Street.

Once again the police received a letter, this time pointing the finger at another doctor, Walter Harper, who had lodged with Cream while completing his studies. This finally established a link with Cream, who was already under surveillance thanks to his unusually detailed knowledge of the killings. Although he had claimed merely to have a professional interest in the medical aspects, Cream had come across as bragging – and once his distinctive, cross-eyed appearance was mentioned by a number of other prostitutes it looked as if the game was up.

Thereafter it did not take long to build a case, particularly when his activities in North America came to light. After being charged and found guilty of the murder of Matilda Clover, Cream was sentenced to hang on 15 November 1892.

To the great disappointment of Londoners, the execution was held inside Newgate rather than in full view of the street, and an angry crowd of 5,000 is said to have gathered outside to protest at being denied such a spectacle. The legend of his last-minute Ripper confession has continued to echo down the years, but that he was in Joliet for the whole of 1888 is well documented, and one can say with certainty that Thomas Neill Cream is definitely not our Jack.

THE BOROUGH POISONER
– OR JACK THE RIPPER? (1902)

GEORGE CHAPMAN, WHOSE REAL NAME WAS Seweryn Antonowicz Klosowski, murdered three women and is yet another frequently cited candidate for the Ripper killings. He enjoyed a substantially longer run at it, however – nearly five years as opposed to Jack's few months – and, as his posthumous reputation as 'the Borough Poisoner' suggests, he preferred an altogether different modus operandi to that of his more celebrated East End rival.

This last point is significant, not least because there is a considerable body of research showing that the majority of serial killers tend to find something that works for them and then stick with it. The Ripper liked to strangle and mutilate prostitutes, whereas Chapman preferred killing barmaids with the poison antimony, and most authorities consider it highly unlikely that Klosowski would suddenly have switched to this means having enjoyed ritually disembowelling his victims on the other side of the river.

Klosowski had first arrived in England some time in the 1880s, a young married Catholic previously apprenticed to a surgeon in Poland but still unqualified and now working as a barber. He briefly relocated again, to the United States, and on returning to London in 1892 was cohabiting with a woman named Annie Chapman, whose surname he decided to adopt.

By 1895 he was married to Mary Spink – both of them bigamously –
and they ran a public house near Old Street called the Prince of Wales.
Mary died on Christmas Day that year, ostensibly of natural causes,
and three years later Chapman married Bessie Taylor. Once again this
was a bigamous arrangement, on his part if not hers.

After a brief stint running a pub in Hertfordshire, the Chapmans
returned to London in 1900 to take over the Monument Tavern in Union
Street, Lambeth – but neither premises nor wife survived the move
for long. Mrs Chapman died barely a year later, on St Valentine's Day,
and shortly afterwards the Monument caught fire suspiciously close
to the date on which Chapman's lease was due to expire.

'I SEE YOU GOT JACK
THE RIPPER AT LAST'

Widowed again, he moved one last time, taking over The Crown public
house at 213 Borough High Street. A few weeks later he announced his
engagement to one of the barmaids, Maud Marsh.

Maud's parents already had reason to be concerned about Chapman,
who had lied to them about another family living above the bar, presumably
in a bid to persuade them that their daughter would be quite safe living on
the premises. Having agreed to this arrangement, they had received a letter
from their daughter suggesting that she would be fired if she did not let
her employer have his wicked way with her, only for this to be followed by
a second letter announcing that she had since married Chapman in secret.

By October 1902, Maud was dead, too, and at this point the suspicions
of a local doctor and the alarm of the Marsh family prompted the police

to make a closer examination of George Chapman's habit of losing wives. On being exhumed, the previous two were found hardly to have decomposed, a peculiarity already recognised as a side-effect of antimony poisoning.

Chapman soon found himself in the dock for murder, and his defence collapsed when he was shown to have purchased quantities of an emetic medicine from a chemist. This was an antimony-rich potassium tartrate compound, known to cause severe paralysis and death if administered in high doses. Duly charged with the third murder, Chapman was convicted on 20 March 1903 and hanged at Wandsworth Prison 19 days later. Unfortunately his motives were never revealed.

Returning to the Ripper rumours, Chapman not only chose a different means to inflict death on his victims but also killed women he knew well, whereas the Ripper almost certainly preyed on strangers. The link between the two has nevertheless proved enduring, depending for the most part on a chance remark from a retired police inspector who congratulated one of Chapman's arresting officers with the words, 'I see you got Jack the Ripper at last.'

The evidence for this is extremely slight, however. Chapman's Polish origins may have led to him being confused with two other Ripper suspects, Aaron Kosminski and Nathan Kaminsky. Or possibly the comment was made in jest and then accepted as fact by a public unable or unwilling to accept that the Ripper was still at large. No serious researchers have given the theory any credence at all, though, and if Jack's true identity is ever discovered it is highly unlikely to be the Borough Poisoner.

Now converted to educational use, although its origins are still clear, the former Crown pub is the only building associated with Chapman to have survived.

NAGGED ALL THE WAY TO
THE GALLOWS (1942)

THE MYTH OF THE BLITZ IS A STRONG ONE, the notion burned into the national psyche that in Britain's hour of direst need, this country's finest hour, we stood alone against the Luftwaffe and the Nazi invader and that Londoners all dug deep and pulled together. In the shadow of the great Dome of St Paul's – wreathed in smoke, rich in symbolism – we snatched victory from the jaws of defeat through a combination of patriotic pride, stoicism, team work, and selfless endeavour.

The reality, inevitably, is rather more complicated and markedly less attractive: spivs thrived as the black market in rationed goods went unchecked; the Royal Family were loudly booed as they toured bomb-damaged streets; houses were looted wholesale; and pedestrians were frequently attacked and robbed under cover of the blackout. With the police so often called away to other duties, crimes generally soared – and in retrospect it seems obvious that even murders would have gone undetected, when air-raids offered so many new ways to conceal a killing and then the body.

On 17 July 1942, for example, a workman helping to demolish the Vauxhall Baptist Chapel just off Kennington Lane lifted a slab and found a body, and it was only natural to assume that it was simply another tragic victim of the air-raid that had taken place the previous October and claimed in excess of 100 lives. Fortunately there were procedures

to be followed even in wartime, and, after the body was examined at the Southwark Mortuary by the Home Office pathologist Keith Simpson, the police were reasonably confident that they were dealing with a murder.

Apart from anything else, the head had been separated from the body, the lower jaw was missing completely, all four limbs had been severed at the elbow or knee, and a blood clot in the throat suggested that the victim had been strangled rather than flattened by falling masonry. There was also evidence to suggest that an effort had been made to further obscure the victim's identity by burning. The pattern of putrefaction seemed out of the ordinary, too, and a search of the burial site revealed the presence of slaked lime, a mixture presumably employed to reduce the odour of a rotting body but which – unlike quicklime – would have inhibited the natural decaying of a corpse.

Back at his laboratory at Guy's Hospital, Simpson was soon able to assert that the body belonged to a woman aged between 40 and 50, who was just over five feet tall and grey-haired. She had, he said, been lying in the crypt of the chapel for between 12 and 15 months. Armed with this information, the police soon came up with a possible identity for the victim: Rachel Dobkin, the estranged wife of an employee in a neighbouring law firm. She had gone missing approximately 15 months previously, matched Simpson's rough description fairly closely, and was subsequently identified using dental records relating to her upper jaw.

Harry Dobkin was arrested shortly afterwards, and a tale emerged of an arranged marriage dating back to 1920. The couple had proved themselves to be incompatible almost immediately, and police heard about years of resentment revolving around the payment of child maintenance for a boy conceived during the three short days they had shared as man and wife. The boy had by now reached his early twenties, and Dobkin –

never particularly regular with his payments – was no longer obliged nor at all keen to continue paying. On several occasions Rachel had attempted to squeeze more money out of him, and four times tried unsuccessfully to sue him for assault. By early April 1941 Dobkin had presumably had enough. After the two of them were observed together on Good Friday at a café in Shoreditch, Rachel was never seen alive again.

Three days later, on the night of the 14 April, there had been a small fire in the Baptist chapel at Vauxhall, which was rather odd as there had been no raid that night. Odder still was that Dobkin – the firewatcher on duty that night – had failed to report it.

With the war on, this was overlooked, and but for the workman's grisly discovery 15 months later Dobkin might have got away with it. Instead he found himself in the dock at the Old Bailey, his barrister striving in vain to convince the jury that the body had been misidentified. Alas for Dobkin, the jury was having none of it, and he was hanged at Wandsworth on 7 January 1943.

The site of the chapel, which stood opposite this charming little courtyard behind St Peter's, Kennington Lane, is now covered by several low-rise blocks of flats.

KING FREDDIE'S
LAST HOURS (1969)

ORCHARD HOUSE, LOWER ROAD, SE16

IT SEEMS REASONABLE TO SUPPOSE that few, if any, citizens of modern-day Uganda are familiar with Lower Road, Rotherhithe. But then the likelihood is that they know about as much about this otherwise-undistinguished corner of South East London than the residents of SE16 knows of Buganda, the largest of the traditional kingdoms of the aforementioned East African republic.

Perhaps they should, though, for it was here at dreary Orchard House that the kingdom's erstwhile ruler – and the sometime President of Uganda – met his end.

The records show that Major General Sir Edward Frederick William David Walugembe Mutebi Luwangula Mutesa II – 'King Freddie' to his friends and to the gossip columnists of Fleet Street throughout much of the 1960s – died of alcohol poisoning, apparently after consuming at least four bottles of vodka in as many hours. Officially the death was taken to be self-inflicted, but four decades on the suspicion still lingers that the exiled former *kabaka*, or ruler of the ethnic Ganda people, was summarily bumped off on the orders of powerful forces back home.

Educated at Magdalene College, Cambridge, and later commissioned into the Army as an officer of the Grenadier Guards, Freddie succeeded to the throne of Buganda on the death of his father in 1939. Over the course of the next 30 years he is thought to have married eleven times and sired

up to 18 children. At the time of his accession Uganda was a British protectorate, but unfortunately Freddie had managed to find himself on the wrong side of both his own people and their colonial overlords within a decade. His followers resented what they saw as his dangerous proximity to the British authorities, and H.M. Government took it badly when he opposed the 1951 proposal to merge the countries of British East Africa – Uganda, Kenya and Tanganyika – into a new federation.

In particular the Ugandans wished to avoid coming under the control of Kenya's white settlers – something similar had already happened in Rhodesia – and things came to a head in 1953 when their *kabaka* was formally deposed by the British Governor, Sir Andrew Cohen, and sent into exile. In fact, as revealed by the *Sunday Telegraph* more than 40 years later, the operation to remove him looked more like a judicial kidnapping, Downing Street dispatching an RAF Handley-Page Hastings transport aircraft to Entebbe with instructions for the crew to bundle Freddie on board and get him out of the country as quietly as possible. The Africans were naturally outraged at Whitehall's high-handed behaviour, and within two years the British authorities here had given in to popular demand and flown Freddie – by now a national hero – back home to be reinstated on his throne.

Freddie's good fortune was not to last long, however. When Uganda was granted independence in 1962, he quickly fell foul of the new ruler, Milton Obote, who initially allowed him to retain a measure of personal prestige but sent him back into exile in 1966. Obote, by now self-declared president, went on to abolish Uganda's sub-kingdoms completely and with them any aspirations to which their ruling families might have clung.

Freddie moved into London's Savoy, where he became something of a minor celebrity, and later to a house in Eaton Place, until what was left of a government allowance was exhausted. Broke, broken down and banned from returning home, King Freddie then removed himself to this anonymous corner of Southwark. By April 1968 – almost exactly two years after he had entertained the Queen Mother, Princess Margaret and Lord Snowdon at his own palace in Kampala – he was reported to be living on the dole, telling the press, 'I'm glad to say the odd friend slips me a fiver now and then.'

'THE WHOLE THING STANK'

On 31 November 1969 poor King Freddie was found dead in the top-floor flat at Orchard House with four empty vodka bottles by his side. Friends refused to believe he had died by his own hand, among them an influential acquaintance from his Cambridge days: the BBC's foreign correspondent John Simpson had visited Freddie the previous day, finding him 'entirely sober and perfectly calm'. As he later recalled, 'I saw no sign of booze in the flat, and I doubt if he could have afforded four bottles of vodka. The whole thing stank.' The finger may have pointed at Obote, but investigations went no further.

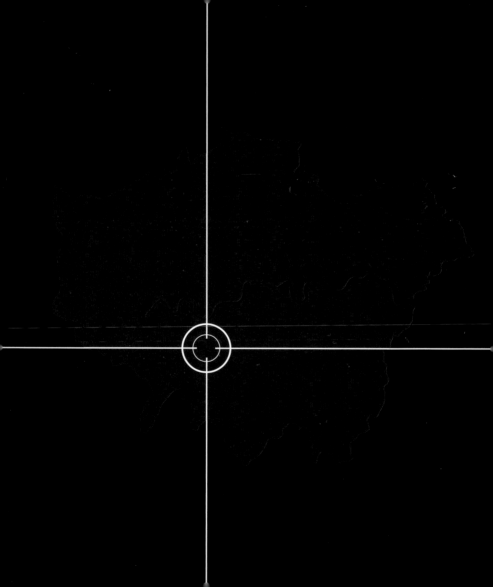

SOUTH WEST LONDON 9

MURDERS OF LONDON

BALHAM'S
BLACK WIDOW
(1876)

A LARGE AND STILL-IMPOSING crenellated Gothic fancy only partially concealed behind blocks of flats, the Priory is one of London's more impressive crime scenes, so it is perhaps appropriate that the evidence of this murder was collected using a genuine silver spoon. The evidence in question was in fact vomit, produced by lawyer Charles Bravo not in court but in bed, for he was himself the victim of this celebrated Victorian poisoning.

In December 1875 Bravo had married a young widow, Florence Ricardo, although it seems that what Bravo found most attractive about her was the considerable fortune she had inherited on the death of Captain Alexander Ricardo, an alcoholic who had been occasionally inclined towards violence. The new arrangement had at first appeared to suit both parties. Florence was able to enjoy the respectability bestowed on her by marriage to a young and thrusting London lawyer, and Bravo could finally leave his parents' home at 2 Palace Green, Kensington, and afford a large house of his own with a staff of twelve.

Four months later, however, Bravo was suddenly taken violently ill, and two days after that – on 21 April 1876 – he was pronounced dead at the age of 28.

Scooped up on the aforementioned spoon, a pool of vomit aroused suspicion, and an autopsy revealed lethal amounts of potassium antimony

in Bravo's body. At the time the compound was a popular emetic, although the quantity indicated that Bravo had almost certainly been poisoned. Suspicion initially fell on his wife, particularly when an examination of Captain Ricardo's corpse revealed traces of the same substance.

But Florence was by no means the only suspect: it soon became apparent that Bravo had acquired more than his fair share of enemies during his short life. Florence's companion Jane Cox was soon in the frame, and so too was a neighbour – Florence's erstwhile lover, the hydropathic pioneer Dr James Gully – as well as a stable-hand who was known to have nursed a grudge against the deceased. Even Bravo himself came under suspicion eventually, the suggestion from Mrs Cox being that he had administered the emetic himself, either in order to commit suicide or by taking an accidental overdose.

At the inquest the jury refused to consider that the young lawyer had committed suicide, however, and the public certainly preferred the idea that he had been bumped off by his wife or her lover, and that a young woman so keen on respectability was not only a murderer but an adulterer to boot.

Unfortunately the case was nowhere near as straightforward as this. Dr Gully clearly had the means and possibly the motive to poison Bravo but not the opportunity – and he had in any case recently ended his relationship with Florence and returned to his wife. Florence certainly had the opportunity to kill her husband but – as far as is known – kept no supplies of the poison at home. And while a conspiracy involving the two of them was certainly suggested at the time, it proved impossible to confirm that any such plot existed.

In the end a second jury was sworn in and the court was forced to accept that the murderer might never be identified. Judge and jury were confident that the victim had been deliberately poisoned using a lethal dose of a dangerous but well known emetic, but the assertion was left to stand that 'there is not sufficient proof to affix the guilt upon any person or persons.'

It was an acquittal of sorts, but with the burden of proof traditionally set much lower in the court of public opinion than would be the case in a court of law, both Gully and Mrs Bravo in the end paid a reasonably heavy price. Four years after the court ruling, Florence apparently drank herself to death; Gully followed her to the grave three years later after being ruined both socially and professionally by the controversy surrounding the case.

Precisely what happened will likely always remain a mystery, but for many the finger still points at the widow with two dead husbands who are known beyond doubt to have consumed exactly the same deadly poison.

CONSPIRACY, COVER-UP
- OR JUST CRIMINAL?
(1911)

CLAPHAM COMMON, SW4

BATTERED TO DEATH near Clapham's magnificent bandstand – the largest and oldest survivor of its type in London – and with a bloody S-shape carved into each cheek, Leon Beron was by most accounts an unsavoury character. He was a small-time slum landlord collecting rents on a few run-down properties in Russell Court near St George's in the East, but talk of his death has rarely moved away from rumours of conspiracies and cover-ups at the highest level.

The grim discovery on New Year's Day 1911 of Beron's poorly concealed body set the scene for one of London's most controversial pre-war murder trials. Believing the killer to be a strong, left-handed man, the police didn't take long finding their suspect: another Jewish emigré of Eastern European origin, Alexander Petropavloff, aka Steinie Morrison, whom witnesses recalled seeing lunching with Beron at the Warsaw kosher restaurant at 32 Osborn Street, E1.

With recent convictions for house-breaking, Morrison was arrested, initially on the convenient grounds that he had moved home without informing the authorities. He was subsequently charged with murder after his picture was identified by a cabbie who claimed to have taken him and a man answering Beron's description from the East End to Clapham. Another cab driver said he had carried Morrison back to Kennington,

while a third, perhaps spurred on by news of a reward being offered by the press, claimed to have driven him back north across the river.

There was also the small matter of a weapon. Morrison had deposited a firearm and a quantity of unused ammunition at the left luggage office of St Mary's, a station on the District line between the present-day Whitechapel and Aldgate East that was closed in 1938 and destroyed during the Blitz.

Morrison insisted he had an alibi, claiming to have been at the Shoreditch Empire the previous evening with 16-year-old Janie Brodsky. He said they were there to see Harry Lauder, apparently the highest-paid performer in the world, and Brodsky confirmed that the tickets had been bought on the door for 1/- apiece. Unfortunately for Morrison theatre staff queried this, pointing out that the tickets that night had been 1/6 and that, with Lauder on the bill, had been sold out well in advance. The court was also told that Morrison would have been familiar with this particular patch of South London, having worked around Lavender Hill.

The evidence against Morrison was circumstantial but nevertheless looked damning, and the collapse of his alibi made his actual conviction a mere formality. A sentence of death was duly handed down – but was almost immediately commuted to life imprisonment by the then Home Secretary, Winston Churchill.

In all likelihood the latter was simply exercising the degree of clemency that his office permitted him, perhaps because the judgement looked shaky and probably was. The defendant and victim had known one another, having been part of the same East End underworld, but there was never any forensic evidence linking Morrison to the murder. Most of the witnesses were decidedly dodgy themselves.

Conspiracy theorists nevertheless had a field day with the case, and they continue so to do. For example, when Beron's body was discovered his wallet was empty: he had clearly been robbed, which could explain the killing. But far more attention has always been paid to his wounds – likened to the f-shaped sound holes on a violin – the suggestion being that the carved 'S' on each cheek proves he was killed by anarchists after being uncovered as a spy. These sinister but unsubstantiated charges were used to link Beron's death with the recent Houndsditch Murders and the Sidney Street siege that followed (p.26). Beron, this argument runs, was a police informant who had been killed for leading the authorities to a team of powerful Latvian anarchists who had broken into a Houndsditch jewellers.

The argument did not prove persuasive at the time, however, and still fails to do so. One is left wondering why an East End villain should go to the trouble of taking another East End villain all the way to Clapham just to finish him off. Morrison certainly continued to protest his innocence but he nevertheless died in prison. Officially his death was put down to his physical state being weakened by repeated hunger strikes, but that has not silenced rumours that he too was bumped off by warders in the pay of someone else.

FREDERICK FIELD,
A VICTIM OF HIS OWN VANITY
(1936)

IN OCTOBER 1931 FREDERICK FIELD, a general handyman employed erecting 'For Sale' boards for a firm of estate agents, visited the premises of a lock-up at 173 Shaftesbury Avenue with his boss. Inside the shop, long since demolished, the two found the body of a 20-year-old streetwalker, Norah Upchurch, who had evidently been strangled a few days previously.

Field came under immediate suspicion, having been at the shop two days earlier. When questioned, he produced a confusing account of how he had lent the shop keys to a stranger with a gold tooth, a man dressed in plus fours who claimed to be an electrician. Field even went so far as to finger a man who was being held in custody, only to see him released shortly afterwards when he turned out not to have any gold teeth.

Somewhat surprisingly Field got away with this, and might have continued to do so were it not for his decision in 1933 to seek fame and fortune by selling his story to a newspaper. The newspaper agreed to buy his neatly written confession, in which Field said he had found Norah Upchurch in Leicester Square, taken her back to the shop, killed her and stolen her handbag. Once published it ran alongside a much larger story examining the possible ramifications of Berlin's Reichstag fire, but it was prominent enough for Field to be re-arrested and charged with murder.

When he withdrew his confession ahead of the trial, however, he appeared once again to have got away with it. In fact the newspapers were used to dealing with cranks who made up stories, and in any case there were a number of inconsistencies in Field's story once it was read more closely. Most obviously he had said he had strangled Upchurch with his bare hands, but marks on the skin of her neck indicated that a belt or cord had been used. Whatever the truth, the judge lost no opportunity in criticising the process of what we know as chequebook journalism. He also felt very strongly that the defendant was a liar and a chancer rather than a murderer, and directed the jury towards a not-guilty verdict. Because of this, Field – who dismissed the unfortunate Upchurch as being of 'disreputable class', i.e. beneath his dignity – walked free once again.

By 1936 Field was living south of the river in Clapham Manor Street, apparently lying low after deserting from the Royal Air Force, which he had joined when he lost his job. By the time he was arrested for this he had already made moves to confess to yet another murder, in an effort to pick up another payment. This time the victim was a middle-aged widow called Beatrice Sutton, whose body, strangled and then smothered beneath a pillow, had been found in her flat at Elmhurst Mansions on 5 April.

Fortunately Field's name still rang a bell in Fleet Street, and he made no real headway with the press before the police began to show some interest. His luck seemed at last to have deserted him third time round, and on 25 April he was formally charged with Sutton's murder. Admitting in interview that he did not know the widow and had no ill feeling towards her, Field claimed to have 'just murdered her because I wanted to murder someone'.

Once again he attempted to withdraw this rather bald confession when brought to the dock in May that year, but the judge was not persuaded by his innocence and neither was the jury. According to contemporary newspaper reports it was thought that Field might deliberately have 'put himself on the spot' as he was tired of living but lacked whatever it took to end it all. On 30 June 1936 the authorities made good that shortfall, if indeed it existed, and Frederick Charles Field was hanged at Wandsworth.

In the absence of a reliable confession it is generally assumed that Field was also responsible for the Shaftesbury Avenue murder, having been crafty enough to insert sufficient inconsistencies into his first newspaper story to ensure that he would not hang for it. In the case of Mrs Sutton he failed to do this, however, seemingly unable to resist inserting a wealth of detail that indicated to the prosecution – even after his denial – that he knew more about the case than any innocent civilian possibly could have.

A DEADLY FARE FOR TAXI DRIVER JACOB DICKEY (1923)

● **BAYTREE ROAD, SW2**

ON 11 JULY 1923 ALEXANDER CAMPBELL 'SCOTTIE' MASON found himself in the dock on a charge of murder, the prosecution seeking to prove that he was responsible for the death of 39-year-old taxi driver Jacob Dickey. The victim had been found dying of gunshot wounds in an undistinguished suburban street running off Brixton's Acre Lane.

Dickey had been driving his fare over from Victoria Station, and had turned off Acre Lane into Baytree Road. Here he was subsequently observed grappling with an unknown assailant before three shots rang out and he collapsed onto the pavement. His attacker made off over a fence into the garden of a property facing onto Acre Lane, now lost beneath a branch of Tesco. He emerged onto the main road through the front door of 15 Acre Lane, leaving behind a pair of gloves, a flashlight and a distinctive cane or swagger stick with an elaborate gold top and a concealed compartment containing writing instruments. Without much difficulty the last object led the CID's Francis Carlin to Eddie Vivian, a known villain sharing digs in Charlwood Street, Pimlico, with a prostititute called Hetty Colquhoun.

Vivian quickly fingered his friend 'Scottie', who he claimed had borrowed the cane while Vivian was ill in bed. Mason had allegedly written to Vivian from prison. 'He wanted me to buy a revolver for him,' Vivian told the police, 'and to have it ready to give him when he came to London on getting out.' The two had agreed to do a house-breaking job together,

but so far Vivian had done no more than obtain a suitable weapon from a dealer he knew south of the river and hand it to Mason.

Mason was soon pulled in for questioning at Brixton police station, and Carlin noticed straightaway that his trousers were torn and that he had scrapes on his hands and knees. Just the sort of minor injuries, in other words, that one might sustain while clambering into someone else's garden in a hurry. Mason admitted that he had indeed got his scratches by clambering over a wall but insisted he had done so elsewhere, possibly Norbury. Unconvinced, Carlin had the two men put into an identity parade. Having been picked out by the woman through whose garden Dickey's killer had escaped, Mason was sent for trial.

'HE WANTED ME TO BUY A REVOLVER FOR HIM'

Carlin would probably have liked to nail Vivian, too, but Hetty Colquhoun's testimony supported his alibi. In his memoirs years later the detective confirmed that, on reflection, he felt 'Vivian had had no hand in the murder of Jacob Dickey, and I felt equally certain that Mason was the guilty man.' Once the case got to court, however, and with Vivian as the chief witness for the Crown, Mason and his barrister A.C. Fox-Davies made strenuous efforts to throw the light onto Vivian, to expose his supposed role in the cabbie's death, and most obviously to shift the blame from the man in the dock to the one in the witness box.

Vivian was clearly a highly undesirable character, one who was entirely happy to purchase a firearm on behalf of an acquaintance newly released from prison, and who at one point had even suggested that

Dickey was a willing participant in the crime. But more compelling than all this was the evidence Carlin had built up against Mason: it was, by his own estimation, 'unassailable'. Vivian, the policeman thought, had nothing to do with the facts of the case against Alexander Mason, and the jury seemed to agree. Mason alone was declared guilty.

There were, even so, a number of contradictions in the case, and not for the first time the Crown had been forced to rely on the testimony of persons whose reputations would ordinarily have rendered their statements suspect. Because of this Mason managed to escape the death penalty, and on being granted a reprieve in 1937 he served with honour in the Merchant Navy but was killed in action.

In light of this, Carlin wisely kept his own counsel on the decision not to hang Mason, instead reserving his final words for the victim. Somehow, he wrote in his memoirs, 'it got about that Jacob Dickey was a straight-up driver, or in other words that he was one of those drivers, of whom there are not a few in the metropolis, who work in connivance with burglars and crooks.' Calling this 'a wicked and outrageous lie', Carlin felt he felt he owed it to the memory of the dead man to make it clear 'that Dickey was an honourable, clean living man' who was murdered by Mason while earning an honest pound.

HENDRICK NEIMASZ,
THE LAST MAN TO HANG
IN LONDON (1961)

HMP WANDSWORTH, SW18

RATHER THAN THE CRIME it is the punishment that most obviously distinguishes 49-year-old Hendrick Neimasz from London's many other murderers. Convicted of killing two people on 12 May 1961 – a Mr and Mrs Hubert Buxton, from Brixton – Neimasz subsequently entered the history books as the last person to be hanged in the capital before the passage of the Murder (Abolition of Death Penalty) Act in 1965.

The execution took place on 8 September 1961 at Wandsworth. The former Surrey House of Corrections had a fearsome reputation for harshness, based in part but not solely on the fact that the warders were still busily birching and flogging criminals until well into the 1950s. Indeed, from 1951 onwards it was the only prison in the country permitted to carry out corporal punishment with such implements, and among those who found themselves at the wrong end of the cat-o'-nine tails were the so-called Mayfair Playboys. This was the gang led by the future 6th Marquess of Bristol, credited with more or less inventing the ram-raid when his black Rolls-Royce was implicated in the theft of artefacts belonging to Henry VIII, Elizabeth I and Anne Boleyn from Hever Castle in Kent.

Wandsworth was also the very last prison in Britain to have its own scaffold. Its role as a place of execution stretched back almost 100 years

to 1878, when the winding down of Horsemonger Lane Gaol in Southwark had required the construction of the charmingly named 'Cold Meat Shed' in a yard at Wandsworth. The guilty were despatched here until 1911, when the gallows was finally moved onto E Wing. Across the river, Pentonville famously boasted a collapsible set of gallows that could easily be shipped by train to wherever they were needed, but the passing of the 1965 Act put an end to this dubious claim to fame. The Wandsworth scaffold, on the other hand, was still being officially checked twice a year to make sure the moving parts were in full working order, and it was not finally dismantled until 1994.

Today, sadly, nothing of it remains. The execution chamber has been converted into a TV lounge for staff, and a few mementoes such as the trapdoor and hangman's lever have been removed to the Galleries of Justice museum in faraway Nottingham.

This is perhaps a shame as, in addition to our double murderer Hendrick Neimasz, the condemned cell has seen off a number of notorious prisoners over the years. These included William Joyce – better known as the Nazi propagandist Lord Haw-Haw, who gouged a swastika into his cell wall – the Acid Bath Murderer (p.114) and Derek Bentley in 1953. In a case that still generates a lot of ill-feeling, the latter was sent to the gallows after the killing of a policeman in Croydon. His accomplice, Christopher Craig, who actually pulled the trigger, was merely jailed as he was under age.

In fact a good deal of debate surrounds many of the executions at Wandsworth. Joyce, for example, was technically not guilty of treason since he was a US citizen and not a British one when he took on German nationality and began his broadcasts. Because of this, the historian A.J.P. Taylor argues that Joyce was, in essence, executed for the very minor offence of making a false statement on a passport. At the same time, many members of the public thought the punishment quite out of proportion for a character widely regarded as something of a joke rather than a serious threat to King and Country.

Others among the 135 who met their ends here certainly were traitors, and chief among them was John Amery. The Old Harrovian son and brother of Members of Parliament, Amery amassed an impressive 74 convictions before joining the Fascist side in the Spanish Civil War. In 1941 he was recruited by the Nazis and began making Hitlerite broadcasts from Berlin, his sincere wish being that he could in this way encourage British internees and PoWs to fight for Germany. Towards the end of the war he switched sides – to support Mussolini – but was captured by Italian partisans and handed back to the British.

During questioning by MI5 in November 1945, Amery became the first person to plead guilty to treason in an English court since the Royalist conspirator Summerset Fox in May 1654. His trial was exceptionally short as a result – just eight minutes – and three weeks later, after greeting the noted hangman Albert Pierrepoint with the words, 'I've always wanted to meet you, though not of course under these circumstances', Amery was dead.

MURIEL MCKAY,
A VICTIM OF MISTAKEN IDENTITY? (1969)

● **20 ARTHUR ROAD, SW19**

MORE THAN 40 YEARS AFTER HER DISAPPEARANCE, Muriel McKay has still not been found. Nor has any evidence emerged to challenge the contemporary assumption that she was taken in error by kidnappers who had actually been after the then wife of media mogul Rupert Murdoch.

Any confusion on this second point is explained by the fact that Muriel was the wife of Alick McKay, Murdoch's deputy chairman at News International. He left for work on 29 December 1969 in Murdoch's blue Rolls-Royce, and returned to Wimbledon that evening to find his neo-Georgian home ransacked and his 55-year-old wife missing. The telephone had been left off the hook and the little piece of card showing the couple's ex-directory number had been prised from the centre of the rotary dial. His wife's overcoat was missing, along with a few bits of jewellery.

Kidnapping of this sort was hitherto unknown in Britain, however, and the police initially assumed Mrs McKay had simply left her husband. They were bemused, to say the least, when McKay called the editor of the *Sun* to get him to run the story of his wife's abduction the following morning.

But within a few hours McKay's suspicions were proven correct when the telephone rang and he was told, 'We are M3 – the Mafia. We tried to get Rupert Murdoch's wife. We couldn't get her so we took yours instead. You

have a million by Wednesday night or we will kill her.' The kidnappers made another two dozen calls over the next few weeks, as well as sending a series of increasingly desperate notes from Mrs McKay, including pieces cut from the green woollen suit she had been wearing on the day of her disappearance.

Gradually a list of instructions was supplied, the first of these requiring Mrs McKay's son to wait in a telephone box on the A10. He was to have a suitcase full of money with him, and a telephone call would tell him what to do next. A policeman posing as Ian McKay duly set off carrying a bag containing mostly false banknotes with a layer of real ones on top. When the call came, he travelled on to another box at High Cross near Ware in Hertfordshire. There, in an otherwise empty cigarette packet, he found a note telling him where to make the 'drop', and his colleagues settled back to watch who came to collect the money. Unfortunately the occupants of a Volvo saloon that had suspiciously been cruising the area spotted the plain-clothes officers and left the scene.

Another drop was hastily arranged, this time further north towards Bishop's Stortford, where the suitcase was again left under close but covert observation. Once again a Volvo was seen circling the area and once again it left without collecting the money, but the police were at least able to get its registration number. This information led them to Rooks Farm in the village of Stocking Pelham, and to brothers Arthur and Nizam Hosein. There was no sign of Mrs McKay at the property but Arthur Hosein's fingerprints were matched to those on the ransom notes and the pair were arrested and charged.

Hosein, it transpired, was something of a fantasist. Long after his conviction he insisted any writer coming to interview him in a top-security mental hospital wear a bowtie. Prior to this, working as a tailor's cutter in Soho, it seems he had conceived a plan to buy some land, live as country gentleman and join the local hunt at Puckeridge. His scheme was proving expensive, however, and the locals refused to treat him like the gentleman farmer he claimed to be. Somewhere along the line he determined that a large injection of cash from Rupert Murdoch would go some way towards solving both problems.

'HAVE A MILLION BY WEDNESDAY OR WE WILL KILL HER'

Given all this it is perhaps hardly surprising that the brothers' defence at the Old Bailey in September 1970 was, like the kidnapping, shambolic and poorly thought-out. Neither confessed but each blamed the other, Arthur further alleging that the whole thing had been masterminded by Murdoch's media rival Robert Maxwell.

The absence of a body necessarily prolonged the time the jury spent on its deliberations but the brothers' guilt was never in much doubt. Arthur Hosein received the maximum sentence of 25 years, with an additional 14 for blackmail and 10 for sending threatening letters, and his brother went down for 15. In court neither revealed what happened to the tragic Mrs McKay.

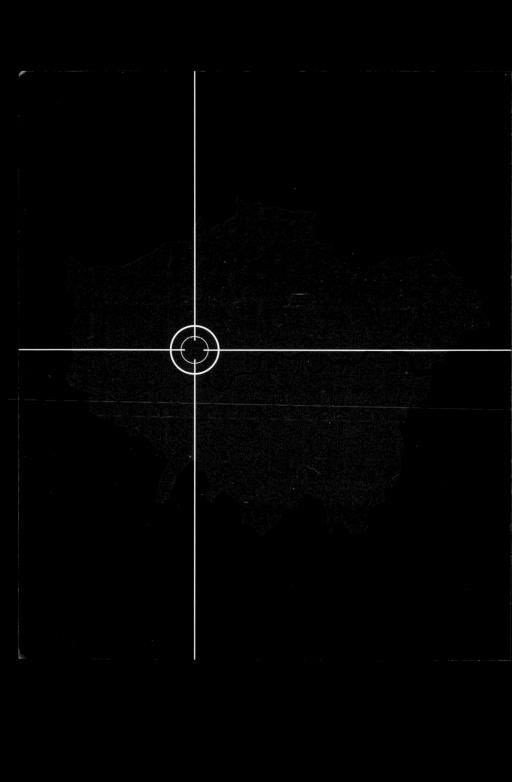

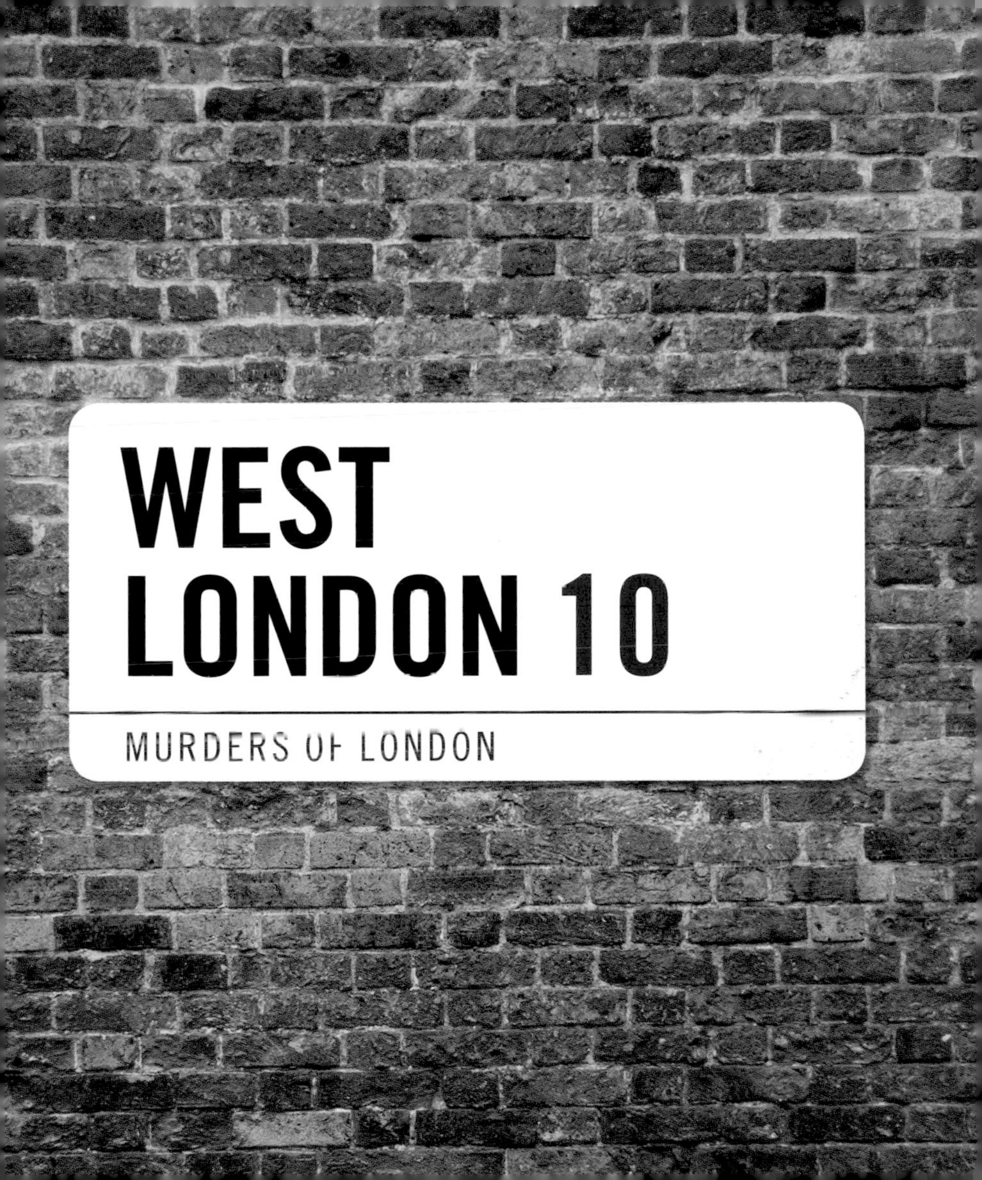
WEST
LONDON 10
MURDERS OF LONDON

WILLIAM WHITELEY'S
BLACK PAST (1907)

● **31–57 WESTBOURNE GROVE, W2**

WHEN EDWARD VII FORMALLY OPENED the City of London's new Central Criminal Court building, a long-overdue replacement for the famously pestilential, rat-infested Newgate Gaol, the inscription carved above the main entrance read: 'DEFEND THE CHILDREN OF THE POOR & PUNISH THE WRONGDOER'. The first murder trial at what quickly became known as the Old Bailey, however, involved the child of a millionaire rather than a poor man – and moreover one who, despite providing a written confession of his wrongdoing *in advance* of his trial, succeeded in escaping the punishment duly handed down by the court.

The man in question was 27-year-old Horace George Rayner. On 24 January 1907 he was charged with shooting dead the self-styled 'Universal Provider' and department store magnate William Whiteley before wounding himself with the same weapon.

The victim, Whiteley, claimed to have arrived in London half a century earlier with only £5 to his name, but by this time his eponymous emporium had grown to occupy an entire row of shops on Westbourne Grove. The move to the present site was still four years away, but business in the 17 departments occupying this row of properties was brisk. The proud boast was that anything could be obtained at Whiteleys, 'from a pin to an elephant', and indeed the January sale was in full swing when a shabbily dressed but formally attired stranger presented himself at the store saying he wished to see the proprietor.

The visitor did not have an appointment, but his request was granted and he was shown into Whiteley's office just before lunchtime. Whiteley lunched punctually at one, so staff were surprised when he came out at four minutes past and asked for a policeman to be summoned before returning to his office and closing the door. Moments later three shots were heard. When the police arrived they found the store owner dead and Rayner on the floor with a bullet through his right eye.

A denial of murder was out of the question, for a note in Rayner's pocket read: "To all whom it may concern: William Whiteley is my father, and has brought upon himself and me a double fatality by reason of his own refusal of a request perfectly reasonable. RIP.'

WHEN DID YOU LAST SEE YOUR FATHER?'

Rayner, it transpired, had told Whiteley that he was his son and that he needed help 'in kind or employment'. When Whiteley asked, 'Is that so? And when did you see me last?' he was told it was many years ago, when the magnate had visited Rayner and his mother in Kilburn. His mother had told him that if he was ever in difficulty he should go and find his 'real father', William Whiteley. With a reputation to protect the 75-year-old Whiteley had flatly refused to offer any assistance to the young man besides suggesting Rayner flee the country.

In court two months later, Rayner, now sporting a glass eye, claimed not to be able to remember exactly what happened next. He was, however, 'jolly glad' that Whiteley was dead, and it took just minutes for the jury to convict him and for the judge to read out a sentence of death

The trial had lasted barely five hours, but the case had gripped the nation as stories emerged of a very different William Whiteley from the 'model employer' image he liked to project. Sharp practices and a bullying manner contrasted strongly with his public persona as an obliging, even obsequious, retailer, but the existence of an illegitimate child surprised few among his workforce, who knew him as a lecherous tyrant who was not above sampling the shop girls as if they were just so much merchandise on his shelves.

Back at the Old Bailey, Rayner's written confession had effectively dashed any hope that he might escape the noose on the grounds of 'impulsive insanity', but Edwardian England saw things very differently and rose up. Persuaded by the somewhat sentimental image of a destitute son spurned by a rich father, petitions poured into the Home Secretary's in-tray – nearly 200,000 signatures were collected in a single week – thanks to which Rayner's sentence was soon commuted to life imprisonment.

Rayner himself always insisted he would have preferred to die, and twice attempted suicide before he was eventually released on licence in 1919. As for Whiteley, he perhaps enjoyed the last laugh, leaving well over £1,000,000 in a will that made no mention of Rayner or his mother. Instead the bulk of his estate went towards securing his reputation as a kindly benefactor, with the purchase of a large patch of freehold land near Walton-on-Thames 'as bright, cheerful and healthy spot as possible . . . and the erection thereon of buildings to be used and occupied as homes for aged poor persons.'

SIX DAYS, SIX ATTACKS, FOUR MURDERS (1942)

- 187 SUSSEX GARDENS, W2
- FLAT 4, 9-10 GOSFIELD STREET, W1
- 153 WARDOUR STREET, W1

FOR A KILLER OR KILLING SPREE to capture the public imagination it always helps if the press can latch onto something memorable, so when Gordon Frederick Cummins was tagged 'the Blackout Ripper' his notoriety was more or less assured.

Even so, press coverage of Cummins's multiple murders and mutilations was nowhere near as extensive as it would have been in peacetime, given the shortage of paper and wealth of more newsworthy incidents brought about by the war. But the war did necessitate the nightly blackouts on which Cummins relied to provide cover for his nocturnal attacks on lone women.

The first attack, or at least the first for which the 28-year-old RAF serviceman is generally held to be responsible, took place on 9 February 1942 in one of three air raid shelters on Montagu Place. The victim was 40-year-old Evelyn Hamilton, described variously as a school teacher and a chemist, whom Cummins strangled before stealing her handbag containing £80.

The following day he struck again: another Evelyn, this time Evelyn Oatey. Cummins cornered the Soho prostitute in her flat at 153 Wardour Street

SUSSEX GARDENS

GOSFIELD STREET

WARDOUR STREET

– a new building on the site now houses offices and an upmarket café – before killing her and slitting her throat with a can opener. From her injuries, police were able to ascertain that the killer was left-handed, and they also picked up a set of finger prints from the weapon. But a change in the killer's modus operandi prevented an immediate connection being made with the previous night's attack.

The following night another prostitute was murdered at 9–10 Gosfield Street, north of Oxford Street. The victim was 42-year-old Margaret Florence Lowe, whom regular punters knew as 'Pearl'. Found in what is still a small but handsome apartment block, she had been strangled with a silk scarf and then mutilated using a razor, inflicting injuries that the pathologist on the case later described as 'quite dreadful'.

By now the police began to suspect they had a savage and highly motivated maniac on their hands, a suspicion that was confirmed just 24 hours later with the discovery of Doris Jannouet's body in her flat at 187 Sussex Gardens. Once again the victim was a prostitute who was known to the police, and once again she had been strangled and mutilated.

The following night brought no news of fresh murders, but 48 hours after that – on St Valentine's Day – Cummins attacked Greta Heywood on St Alban's Street just off Piccadilly Circus, where the pair had been for a drink. Heywood was fighting off her attacker when they were disturbed by a delivery boy, and Cummins took off down Haymarket. Unfortunately for him, he had dropped the case containing his gas mask during his escape. Together with his would-be victim's description, the serial number stencilled on the side of the case – 525987 – led police right to him, albeit not before he had attempted yet another attack on a woman near Paddington station.

Cummins was traced to his billet in St John's Wood, where detectives subsequently found personal effects belonging to some of his victims. He was questioned about four murders and two attempted murders. Although Cummins had occasionally represented himself falsely as the illegitimate son of a peer, he had no previous convictions, but the evidence against him was strong – conspicuously so in the case of Evelyn Oatey, as his prints matched those found on the tin opener at her flat.

For this reason, and with police resources more than usually stretched in wartime, further enquiries were suspended. The Blackout Ripper was charged with just the one murder and the case was heard at the Old Bailey on 27 April 1942. A defence of sorts was mounted, but to little avail: the trial lasted barely an hour and the jury took just 35 minutes to find Gordon Frederick Cummins guilty as charged.

According to legend, Cummins's hanging at HMP Wandsworth on 25 June coincided with another air raid over London.

WHERE IS
10 RILLINGTON PLACE?
(1943-53)

ORNAMENTAL GARDEN BETWEEN NOS. 9 AND 10 BARTLE ROAD, W11

SEARCHERS AFTER HERCULE POIROT'S ADDRESS will look in vain for
Whitehaven Mansions or Sandhurst Square; while Sherlock Holmes
enthusiasts will find something at 221b Baker Street, the sad reality is
that Conan Doyle fixed on that particular address for his famous detective
at a time when the house numbers petered out at 85. Occasionally things
happen the other way round, however, and genuine addresses disappear
just as quickly as fictional ones spring to life. Of these, one of the most
famous is almost certainly 10 Rillington Place, a run-down terraced house
in a small cul-de-sac, which was literally wiped off the map after the truth
emerged about its most famous resident, serial strangler John Christie.

As a result, few locals are entirely sure where Rillington Place once
was, something that might have pleased their 1950s predecessors, scores
of whom were understandably miffed at the street's notoriety and
thoroughly fed up with gawpers coming to nose around. After Christie's
execution in 1953 for the murder of at least six women, they petitioned
the local council to do something about it. Initially the 1860s cul-de-sac
was simply renamed Rushton Close, after a nearby mews of that name.
(Rushton Mews still exists, and is frequently mistaken for Rillington
Place.) As Rushton Close it lasted barely 20 years, as both it and the
surrounding area were levelled for redevelopment in the mid-1970s.

At that stage it seems plausible that a decision was taken deliberately to obscure the crime scene. Christie ought by then to have been old news, but his story had been refreshed in 1961 by Ludovic Kennedy's magisterial book *10 Rillington Place*, and then again 10 years later by an excellent film version starring Richard Attenborough and John Hurt. Focusing on the wrongful execution of Timothy Evans for Christie's crimes, Kennedy's book was to have far-reaching implications: the notorious case contributed in large part to the abolition of capital punishment for murder in 1965. But perhaps it had an effect here, too, for a glance at the orientation of Lancaster Road, Bartle Road, St Andrew's Square and Wesley Square shows no real commonality or shared boundaries with the former Rillington Place.

IT WON'T BOTHER YOU FOR LONG'

Instead of following the old layout, the lines of flats and houses south of this stretch of the Circle Line seem very purposefully to have been positioned in such a way as to conceal the precise position of no.10. None of the new addresses matches it exactly. In fact, as near as one can judge, the plot of no.10 is probably now occupied by the small ornamental garden located between the two addresses mentioned above.

It is of course tempting to wonder how bad a murderer has to be for the scene of his crimes to be completely obliterated in this way, and if Christie's example is anything to go by the answer seems to be: very bad indeed.

Injured by gas in the First World War and briefly a special constable in the Second, John Christie had a history of petty criminal behaviour long before killing his first victim – a munitions worker and part-time prostitute – in 1943. Favouring a combination of domestic gas (which at this time was highly toxic), rape while the victim was unconscious, and eventually strangulation, Christie's habit was to conceal his victims in the garden and house at 10 Rillington Place.

In 1948 the bodies of the wife and baby of a fellow tenant, Timothy Evans, were found in an outside wash-house. Both had been strangled. Christie was called as witness for the prosecution after the somewhat simple-minded Evans had confessed to the crimes under heavy police questioning. He subsequently changed his story and repeatedly claimed Christie was the murderer, but he was nonetheless hanged at Pentonville on 9 March 1950.

Christie sensibly bided his time for the next few years, but in December 1952 he killed his wife and emptied her bank account, managing to explain away her disappearance to anyone who enquired. Then, between January and March 1953, he dispatched three more victims in his usual manner.

Christie's activities only came to light when new tenants at 10 Rillington Place peeled away some old wallpaper to reveal a cavity containing three trussed-up bodies. By now Christie had quit the property and fled, but he was recognised by a police constable on Putney Bridge and quickly confessed to six murders. On 15 July 1953 he was hanged for one of them: that of his wife, Ethel. The story goes that, while waiting for the drop with his arms pinioned, Christie complained that his nose was itching. Albert Pierrepoint was able to assure him, 'It won't bother you for long.'

NEITHER AN OFFICER NOR
A GENTLEMAN (1946)

PEMBRIDGE COURT HOTEL, 34 PEMBRIDGE GARDENS, W2

AFFECTING THE STYLES AND TITLES of the officer class but emphatically no gentleman, Neville George Clevely Heath used his good looks and charm to deadly effect as he progressed from deserter through fraudster to sadistic double murderer.

The product of an undistinguished private school in Surrey – his father, a barber, had scrimped and saved to find the fees – Heath joined the RAF in 1937 but was soon discharged after going AWOL from No.9 Squadron at Duxford. Thereafter he spent a similarly brief period in borstal, convicted of a number of charges including obtaining credit by deception and housebreaking.

Following the declaration of war in 1939, Heath joined the Royal Army Service Corps but his second spell under orders was no more successful than his first. He fled to Johannesburg and signed on with the South African Air Force, where he was promoted to captain but subsequently court martialled for wearing medals to which he was not entitled and shipped back home to London.

On 20 June 1946, Heath – now in the habit of using a number of different aliases including Group Captain Rupert Brooke and Lieutenant Colonel Armstrong – checked in to 34 Pembridge Gardens, the Pembridge Court Hotel at the time. Signing the register with his own name but appending a suitably impressive-sounding military rank, he was given

The Royal Borough of Kensington
and Chelsea
PEMBRIDGE
GARDENS. W.2

the key to room 4 before leaving to meet a companion, Mrs Margery Gardner, at the Trevor Arms in Knightsbridge.

In theory Gardner's masochistic tastes should have sat comfortably with Heath's sadistic tendencies, and indeed the pair had caused some concern at the Strand Palace Hotel in February of that year, when suspicious noises coming from a bedroom had prompted the manager to burst in. The 32-year-old film extra had refused to make a formal complaint, however, and four months later was evidently perfectly happy to be seen back in Heath's company.

'PUT ME DOWN AS NOT GUILTY, OLD BOY'

Back at Pembridge Court, the couple had still not checked out by 2pm, so a chambermaid let herself into the bedroom. Heath was gone and Gardner was dead on the bed with visible bite and whip marks and what a post mortem revealed to be ferocious internal injuries. These had been inflicted using a short poker that lay in the fireplace, and her face appeared to have been licked clean of blood.

By the time the body was discovered, Heath had left London for Bournemouth, where a 'Group Captain Rupert Brooke' checked in to the Tollard Royal Hotel (now apartments). He dined here with 21-year-old Doreen Marshall, whom he had met in a neighbouring hotel, and who was reported missing the following day. Heath helpfully identified her in a police photograph but claimed no knowledge of where she might be.

Fortunately, Detective Constable Souter recognised his informant from a picture circulated by Scotland Yard, and asked the group captain whether he was not in fact called Heath. This was denied, but a search through his coat pockets revealed a left-luggage ticket leading the officers to a suitcase containing various of his personal effects – including a riding crop that was matched to Margery Gardner's appalling injuries.

Even without the subsequent discovery of Doreen Marshall's body hastily hidden beneath a hedge, it was a relatively open-and-shut case. In court on 24 September 1946, the accused was inclined to plead guilty until his brief questioned the wisdom of doing so with a capital crime. 'Alright,' Heath is reported to have said, 'put me down as not guilty, old chap.'

Really only one question remained to be answered – was Heath insane? – but the verdict of two prison doctors that he was quite sane left him no escape route. On 16 October 1946, after requesting a whisky ('better make it a double'), Heath was hanged at Pentonville by Albert Pierrepoint.

In 1980 Heath enjoyed a kind of second life when he was portrayed by the late Ian Charleson in *The Ladykillers*, and a few years after that he was said to have inspired the Nigel Havers character 'Ralph Gorse' in the television series *The Charmer*.

HARRY ROBERTS,
POLICE KILLER (1966)

HARRY ROBERTS WAS A CAREER CRIMINAL who started young, selling ration books and black market goods for his mother. He served time in Gaynes Hall borstal, a building that had been home to Oliver Cromwell three centuries previously and had more recently housed a branch of the wartime Special Operations Executive. Subsequent National Service with the army in Malaya taught Roberts the means to kill.

Once demobbed, Roberts quickly moved into armed robbery, joining a gang that targeted bookies, banks and offices. In 1959 he escaped the noose by the narrowest of margins when one of the gang's victims died of his injuries a year and three days after being attacked. This was two days outside the period in which Roberts could have been charged with murder, and instead he received a seven-year custodial sentence. The victim on that occasion had been hit hard with a glass decanter, but it was through his subsequent reliance on guns that Roberts gained his reputation as a police killer, a habit for which he went on to serve one of the longest prison sentences of any British criminal.

On 12 August 1966, a sunny Friday, Detective Sergeant Christopher Head, Detective Constable David Wombwell and PC Geoffrey Fox were sitting in an unmarked police car on the unremarkable-looking Braybrook Street, on the edge of Wormwood Scrubs. They were on the lookout for car thieves known to be operating in the area, unaware that, in a van parked a few

HERE FELL
PS
CHRISTOPHER HEAD
PC
GEOFFREY FOX
PC
DAVID WOMBWELL
12th AUGUST 1966

yards away from them, Roberts and two accomplices were 'tooled up' and planning the theft of a number of fast getaway cars for a robbery in Northolt.

The thieves' old Standard Vanguard was noticeably decrepit, smoking badly and clearly untaxed, so Head and Wombwell went to investigate. As they were searching the van, Roberts, perhaps nervous about what they might find, shot both men with a 9mm Luger, one through the eye and another in the head. Meanwhile his accomplice, John Duddy, had approached the unmarked car and shot Fox twice at point-blank range. The site is now marked by a small but dignified memorial on the Scrubs side of the road.

'I JUST REACTED AUTOMATICALLY. I WENT ON TO AUTOPILOT'

According to Roberts himself, what became known as the Massacre of Braybrook Street was 'all over in 30 seconds . . . I just reacted automatically. I went on to autopilot.' Nor did it take long for those responsible to be captured: a tip-off led police to the second accomplice, Jack Witney, who provided names and addresses for the other two. Duddy was arrested two days later in Glasgow, while Roberts went on the run. He was captured after one of the biggest police manhunts in British history tracked his progress through Epping Forest to a makeshift camp on the Herts-Essex border.

The triple killing had horrified the public and the jury took barely half an hour to find all three men guilty. Execution was no longer possible – the death penalty had been abolished just eight months before – but the trial judge Mr Justice Glyn-Jones recommended that the three serve a minimum of 30 years each, telling Roberts he thought it unlikely that any future Home Secretary would 'ever think fit to show mercy by releasing you on licence'.

Duddy was sent to Parkhurst, where he died in 1981. Witney was controversially released on licence five years after his imprisonment, only to meet an appropriately violent end when he was bludgeoned to death by an associate with a hammer. Roberts remained inside, however, lending weight to the theory that Home Secretary James Callaghan had had Roberts in mind when he promised the 1967 Police Federation Conference that, 'because of the abolition of capital punishment, some murderers now in prison will die in prison.'

But in February 2009, reports in the press suggested that Roberts was now being considered for parole. Unsurprisingly the Police Federation was among those who complained, its chairman expressing his horror that such a move was being contemplated for a 'monster [who] has never expressed a word of contrition'. On the contrary, insisted Paul McKeever, 'in prison he developed his artistic skills. He painted pictures showing police officers being killed. He was also well known in the prison community for his baking skills. He baked pies with designs on the crusts that pictured police being killed . . . He should stay where he belongs. Decent society does not deserve the displeasure of his company.'

As for Prisoner 231191 himself, he told the *Independent* newspaper that, after 42 years banged up, he was no longer Harry Roberts the police killer, just Harry Roberts the 73-year-old pensioner. 'Of course I regret what happened and I wish I could turn the clock back,' he said, 'but I can't. It's something that happened in a few seconds, but has changed so many people's lives.'

THE BRUTAL KILLING OF
OSSIE CLARK (1996)

PENZANCE STREET, W11

IMMORTALISED IN A CELEBRATED HOCKNEY PORTRAIT that hangs in
Tate Britain and patronised by the likes of the Beatles, Jimi Hendrix
and Twiggy, fashion designer Raymond 'Ossie' Clark was proof for the
young Derek Jarman that decadence was 'the first sign of intelligence'.
Unfortunately Clark's descent into obscurity and poverty was, if anything,
even more spectacular than his rise to sixties stardom.

In the mid-1960s Clark had been dubbed the 'King of the King's
Road' by the fashion press, and considered himself to be 'as famous
as egg foo yong'. Meeting the zeitgeist head-on with chiffons, snakeskins
and op-art funware described by one commentator as 'sex incarnate',
he quickly became both a fan and an intimate of rock's aristocracy.
His precipitate decline was such that some years earlier, when a *Daily
Mail* reader had written in asking, 'Whatever happened to Ossie Clark?'
it was left to Clark himself to write in with an answer. Describing
his marriage break-up and how he lost his love of fashion, Clark
admitted that he had financial difficulties and had been seeking
'more genuine values' to replace what he called his 'previous
somewhat unreal lifestyle'.

Clark ascribed his success to 'my brain and my fingers' but, perhaps
unsurprisingly, sex and drugs had also played an important role in his
life. After separating from his wife and business partner Celia Birtwell

in 1974, the 32-year-old Royal College of Art graduate had then embarked on a series of gay relationships.

By 1987 he was reduced to living partly by barter, producing designs for friends and others in return for free holidays, a sofa to sleep on and, on one occasion, the settling of a bill for the repair of his sewing machine. Living in much-reduced circumstances, he finally moved into a tiny council flat in Penzance Street with the Department for Health and Social Security footing the bill.

Whilst doubtless something of an oddball in such an environment, Clark is still remembered with warmth and affection by some of his neighbours, one of whom described his flat as 'organised chaos and artistically neglected'. Clark still allowed himself the odd flight of decadent fancy when this was possible – spare cash would go on multi-coloured Sobranie cocktail cigarettes – but he quickly became deflated if anyone raised the subject of his once-stellar career.

Occasionally it looked as though he might recover some of his early flair: he successfully trained Bella Freud to pattern cut, produced a couple of small collections for the manufacturer Alfred Radley, and would now and again produce one-off designs for close friends. After his death a neighbour recalled a visit by Bianca Jagger to Penzance Street a few months previously, but such activity was clearly never more than sporadic.

In February 1996 Clark escaped a prison sentence 'by the skin of my teeth' after crashing into a police car and assaulting one of its occupants. Just six months later his erratic life came to a shuddering halt. At 6am on 7 August, Clark's 28-year-old lover, Diego Cogolato, dialed 999 and told the operator he thought he might have killed somebody. When police gained access to Clark's flat they found the 54-year-old's body on the floor, his skull smashed and his body bearing the marks of 37 stab wounds.

In court Cogolato admitted manslaughter on the grounds of diminished responsibility. He was jailed for six years after what was described as a 'transient psychotic episode' in which he believed his former lover was the devil. It was, said the judge Mr Justice Douglas Brown, 'a frenzied attack, while you were in a psychotic state which may have been brought on by a combination of drugs, both prescribed and illicit'.

'AS FAMOUS AS EGG FOO YONG'

A decade earlier, during one attempted comeback, Ossie Clark had been all but ignored by the press, despite catwalk appearances by Marie Helvin and Jerry Hall. But his violent death changed all that, and once again he was front-page news. Prices of his vintage pieces climbed rapidly, and in July 2003 queues formed at the V&A for a retrospective showing his best work. Ossie, posthumously but undeniably, was back on centre stage.

Dying for more?

WWW.MURDERSOFLONDON.COM